Black Elk's
LIFE SPEAKS
"That Much...More"

MICHAEL W. TAYLOR
University of Mary

Kendall Hunt
publishing company

Contents

Acknowledgments

When it comes to knowledge that is culturally responsive in nature, the most authentic origin of such knowledge comes from stories forged through relationships. This book was initially guided by traditional scholastic canon often suffocated by the academy. Yet, with the impact that serious consideration of Indigenous scholarship can have on the soul of a scholar—or at least this author—the course of this endeavor changed completely, and thankfully so. Such a change in course, which can only come from a broad Indigenous understanding of language tethered as an umbilical cord, has transformed my scholarship and ultimately my way of living. If only this change could have come earlier in life, nevertheless, due to seminal experiences like the Dakota Access Pipeline Protest (DAPL) coming more mid to my life span, so did (finally) a sense of visionary pragmatism realized and linked together in a previous book written, *Perpetuating Joy in Affinity Spaces Through Intercultural Pedagogy.*

Chance encounters with the people over the years, since I have arrived with my family on the Great Plains, have become less romanticized and more real in terms of fundamental human relationships. Relationships with foundational qualities of dignity and worth ground relations in which strikingly I have been reminded of by *Mitákuye Oyás'iŋ*—all are related. No doubt the qualities and realizations aforementioned here and throughout the remainder of the book have been an impetus and inspiration. While Black Elk is central to this book, and his saintly and holy life as a healer is to be thanked for this book's evolution from traditional scholarly canon to allowing for his life to speak "that much…more," there are also others to acknowledge for such an evolution. First and foremost, I thank Maka Black Elk, who is a descendant of Black Elk and someone I feel will someday be another installation of seminal Lakota people written about regarding ways in which one's life can speak as a cultural bearer, educator, mystic, and in today's context, also as cultural healer.

There are so many people with Indigenous roots whom I want to list here. Given their review of this book, they may not see themselves in print but hopefully understand their influence was replete in this book's construction. If there is any consolation, those not explicitly listed here will implicitly find resonance with the following who have led me in my fifth decade of life. In this stage of life, I'm finally listening (as the Benedictines would say with the ear of one's heart), to the true voices speaking, like Black Elk himself, and those who share his familial lineage and cultural heritage as exceptional people well before my own ancestors who came from Western Europe. Dr. Carmelita Lamb is someone who came into my life, along with the rest of my University of Mary colleagues, who figuratively and literally saved my life. Carmelita ventured with me on so many journeys to places initially unfamiliar to me, yet she risked my unfamiliarity with her fellow Indigenous people, seeing something in me I had yet to discover in terms of embracing my place with those all related. I am grateful to her and my colleagues for the grace to allow me to venture to places as politically tenuous as DAPL, and other Native Nations, in an attempt to share with undergraduate and graduate students, these experiences and more broadly in wounded places like Northern Ireland. There are additional people hailing from the Oceti Sakowin and other Native Nations like Denny Gayton, Dakota Goodhouse, Bobby Grey Eagle, David Archambault, Jr., Scott Davis, Sashay Schettler, Travis Albers, and numerous Native graduate students who often make up half of our graduate education program at the University of Mary.

Overall, thank-you to the people of Native Nations I have spent considerable time learning from and listening to: Standing Rock, Turtle Mountain, and Pine Ridge. I would be remiss if I didn't mention explicitly those who have been formative with this book's construction, who do their best to be allied with Native people. Drs. Peter Huff and Damian Costello, along with retired archivists and scholar Mark Theil, and Father Michael Steltenkamp, have often been my sounding board and guided me carefully as I have migrated to this sense of Indigenous scholarship as primary, and non-Native secondary, essentially flipping what has traditionally been the canon—at least in works associated with Black Elk. I continue to cherish the wise, frank, counsel of Erik Holland and his cohort of colleagues associated with the North Dakota Heritage Center and Museum and North Dakota Humanities Council, along with various historically and culturally rich resources available due to noble staff at the many North Dakota State Parks and historical/cultural locations near and far.

Thank you for those present-day missionaries on Pine Ridge, Turtle Mountain, and Standing Rock like Monsignor Chad Gion, Fathers Michael and David, Father Doust, Deacon Bill White, and countless other religious people: priests, sisters, and lay missionaries like the Jesuits, and SOLT—you know who you are! While many of the above-mentioned people are associated with the Catholic Church—and no doubt the Church bears its blemishes alongside current progress—I as a Catholic convert am grateful for the daily witness while accompanying Native people, realizing the steep hill of historical trauma to ascend often triggered and causing difficulty in terms of their respective ministry. While many of us have the luxury to place ourselves in and outside some of these environments that may someday be impacted by the hopeful canonization of the Servant of God Black Elk, the present-day Catholic, Protestant, and other missionaries bear the cross to carry in terms of any collateral impact relative to Black Elk's canonization. If anything, those directly accompanying the people of various Native Nations in a ministerial role is the reason why getting such a canonization like Black Elks is as genuine and familiar as possible in terms of his life speaking "that much…more."

At the risk of coming short in this litany of acknowledgments, ending with origin seems proper and fitting. Educator and philosophy Parker Palmer, along with my doctoral committee, namely my chair Dr. Randall Koetting, modeled the courage to not only advocate publicly for learning and learners, but also guided me back to myself. Parker Palmer's seminal work *Let Your Life Speak* became the framework that finally salvaged my numerous failed attempts to complete my doctoral dissertation. Randy Koetting witnessed my coming of age via my autoethnography as I outlined my entire dissertation on panels of whiteboards, and then to his horror, I nearly erased the outline without any other reference to formal notes, other than what was emblazoned in my brain or more accurately, the soul crowded out by an ego that initially thought my memoirs were sufficient for doctoral caliber research. It was this *Autoethnographic Journey to the Self* (originally soul…see, a bit of an ego remains), that allowed me to not only see my true self in all its glory AND infamy, but also see those I encountered from the comfortable beginnings in segregated suburbia to presently in the Great Plains of North Dakota. As arduous a process that a dissertation can be, so is the process of revising, editing, and revising again, as goes with the writing of academic papers and now a second book. Since my ego has been defeated more or less by my true self as it is in relation to others, there is no doubt more acceptance and grace to those who've aided in the endeavor to edit past and present scholarly endeavors: namely my neighbor and scholar in her own right, Carrie, who edited papers foundational to this book and a previous book with Kendall Hunt Publishing (KH). Specifically, I am thankful to Sam, Sheri, and Jen at KH for their patience, guidance, and professionalism.

Overall, it is this consistent process of seeing myself fully via scholarship, prayer, reflection, and being simply engaged with others and the beauty of the environment, that have allowed me to better see all who make up a sense of humanity with dignity and worth. Dignity and worth are not things I can bring to others; they are already present, which has prompted a kind of dispositional relationship that has made all the difference, in particular with those from a whole host of Indigenous communities who are often, as Anton Treuer would remind, often imagined and rarely understood. No doubt, we are fully blessed with knowledge both virtual and otherwise to imagine the other, that it is indeed time to understand and heal interculturally. Thank-you to Anton for his continued guidance, insight, and attestation as a cultural bearer, so much so that it extends even to this kid originally from the segregated suburbs of the broader Detroit Metropolitan area.

Often, as I have learned in painstaking fashion at times, healing begins at home. And in the home I come home to, gratefully, cupboards are stocked, a refrigerator is stocked, and multiple bedrooms remain for family, countless friends, missionaries, academics, activists, and yes at times those very new to our family. Healing is only meaningful to the broader community if I am about it under our own roof. This process of being about healing started under the roof first built by my father and mother, Rod and Phyllis Taylor, along with an amazing, blended family of brothers and sisters I still am fortunate to have living today. And while John, Kathy, Nancy, Rick, and Dick navigated their own eras of challenge and triumphs, they imparted on their little brother the value of family, no matter how the family was formed, or malformed at times. What a joy it has been to celebrate the mosaic of family ties that have broadened from our initial six "Brady Bunch"-like family to nieces, nephews, grandchildren, cousins, and in-laws to name a few. If this cup of joy, in terms of family were enough, and if I'm patient enough to take stock with gratitude that cup overflows, reminiscent of a wedding blessing, said by a Catholic priest, for longevity of life for one's children and children's children. Then in fact, total bliss has arrived in our grandson Theodore Ronald Taylor. Yes, one blessing after another as "Theo" has come to our family from his father, our son August, and daughter-in-law, Rachel. While composing a book, with potential of magnitude and levity, at least when trying to offer something to a wounded world in need of cultural healing, hope comes in all shapes and sizes, including this grandson who is surrounded by two sets of grandparents, and August's additional sisters-in-law, along with his brothers Douglas and Michael and sister Frances.

Finally, my life and all the mounting gratitude would be sparse if it weren't for my wife of thirty-plus years, Kate. Kate and her large Catholic family were often my respite and refuge when I was away from my immediate family. Most often authors who pen such books as this are historians, theologians, or maybe even anthropologists or sociologists, but educators? Yes, often I have wondered whether I should return to my "lane" or "wheelhouse" of research; nevertheless, when I met Kate Mancl, I fell in love quickly with someone who had woven, and continues to weave, a deep and abiding faith life into all facets of life, for all that she encounters. Along with my zeal for the Liberal Arts, Kate taught me that the integrated, virtuous life is not reserved for only those with a specialty of knowledge. In fact, such a life is fully lived by those who see the fullness of life as it is gifted by others in a free exchange, freely gifted first by a loving God. This I have learned from Kate who was and continues to be my gateway to God. I hope to offer this book, which has no doubt taken time away from some of our walks, talks, and night time Netflix or Amazon binges, as some small token of my love and appreciation for her witness and affirmation of a loving God to all people she encounters, myself included. Through her, people are reminded of being perpetually loved by God.

Foreword

Nicholas Black Elk's process for canonization as a Catholic Saint had surfaced almost out of nowhere for me. I was personally in the dark in the earliest stages of it. However, as soon as the committed Lakota Catholic leaders and other family members of Black Elk began this endeavor and succeeded in the effort to get Black Elk officially recognized as a Servant of God, the floodgates opened. Prior to that, I had not spent a lot of time thinking about Black Elk as a saint. Or what that might mean for me, my family, my tribe, and the Catholic Church.

I first met Dr. Mike Taylor like how a lot of people met during the pandemic, through video and phone calls as we were confined to our homes and offices. Dr. Taylor reached out to me to hear my perspective on Black Elk, his life, and his potential for sainthood. What occurred over the years was a plethora of conversations that spanned far beyond the original interest in Black Elk, but in the myriad ways in which his life, story, and his journey might still be relevant for us today. Our conversations about Black Elk brought new interpretations in my own experience as a descendant of Black Elk and one who has heard, throughout my life, stories of him.

While growing up, Black Elk was both a mystery and incredibly familiar. Being the descendant of someone as famous as he has not always been welcome in my life. Through this journey of speaking with Dr. Taylor, and pulling apart my thoughts on Black Elk, I gained a new relationship with him as an ancestor. In many ways, he became more real than I'd ever thought of him before this point. Through this work written by Dr. Taylor I feel even more connected as his life comes to life across the pages through the ways his impact on my community continued.

Dr. Taylor has written a rich and nuanced exploration of Black Elk and the ways in which his life both serves as a fountain of spiritual strength and as a complex figure perhaps born far before his time. Weaving in stories from multiple authors, family members, and interviews, Dr. Taylor illuminates the challenge that Black Elk gives to our community today. We are a people fraught with varying battlefields drawn along the lines of identity. Black Elk is both an embodiment of that battlefield and a testament to a way forward. Dr. Taylor balances this analysis well and brings forward the lingering questions that make Black Elk's life not only salient for today's audience but also in a way that allows his life to say "that much…more."

Maka Akan Najin Black Elk

Introduction

Bookshelves and web-based sources are replete with accounts of seminal Lakota mystic and healer Black Elk. So why another accounting of Black Elk? The assumption of this book is that while the cannon of Black Elk literature is established, there would appear to be a gap in terms of the way in which Black Elk's life speaks through his familial descendants, who when consulted about what has been written about Black Elk, due to their knowledge of stories based on familial accounts of Black Elk, stipulated his life speaks "that much ... more."

This book intended to explore "that much ... more" relative to the way in which Black Elk's life speaks, via a research endeavor that integrated personal narrative and participant researcher interviews and experiences, with foundational/historical and contemporary, researched sourced materials. An example of foundational research contextualizing this book is nearly two years of interviews with Black Elk's great-great-great grandson, Maka Black Elk, highlighting historical, anthropological, and contemporary perceptions of Black Elk in particular, and Native people in general. Finally, the book culminated by considering the implications of how Black Elk's life continues to speak, in the face of historical trauma, survivance, and cultural healing, through additional familial and related stories, as the educator, culture bearer, and "old man" dreamer and visionary.

NEXUS OF PERSONAL LIFE JOURNEYS AND PERSONAL PREFACE

Personal life journeys have a way of unintentionally finding a collective nexus, particularly when the journey seemed to have a sense of consistent clarity, some in the psychoanalytic world like Jung would call this synchronicity. One such unexpected, even paradoxical congruence includes the primary subject of this book Black Elk, his great-great-great grandson Maka, and me as the author.

In retrospect, the ways in which these three people's life journeys have crossed seem clearer due to stories of spiritual formation and plight. This is by no means to suggest that the three have experienced the same journey. Rather, when each journey is given the opportunity to speak for itself, in relation to other lives afforded the same emancipatory support, then context and complexity can deepen, connect, and at times even distort a sense of intercultural affinity. This affinity, upon closer consideration, would appear to be more of a positive inclination to the other, and when such affinity is given space to flourish, this nexus becomes more evident (Taylor, 2019, 2021).

For myself, a complex, even painful, autoethnographic journey to the self, by means of a dissertation research endeavor, provided the foundation for a positive juncture with unlikely "others." Though some may wonder how a self-study could structure a doctoral dissertation, those who have knowledge about this process vicariously via words written or directly by the author have seen that it is akin to peeling an onion to the core of one's most authentic self. The onion of my layered life was left open for those reading the dissertation study and subsequent publications, beginning with a *personal preface* (Taylor, 2012). In terms of *personal preface*, Douthat's (2018) bravery and courage, as an author, to stand in the face of publishing pressure and advocate for such a personal beginning is helpful company for those who believe that such an approach is

> a story that cannot be written about neutrality … So it makes sense at the onset to briefly lay out my own background and biases, the experiences and assumptions that I bring to telling of this very fascinating and very much unfinished story. (p. xi)

Within the context of my own background, biases, experiences, and assumptions as the author of this book, also brought to telling of this fascinating and very much unfinished story are scholars such as Michael Steltenkamp (2009, 1993, 1983), who also experienced a personal nexus journey with Black Elk; illustrating "how the legacy of stereotypes … inherited obscures the flesh-and-blood individuals who are Native people." And like his journey, his focus on the life of Black Elk by means of his direct association with Black Elk's descendants, namely daughter Lucy, revealed a man "who has been characterized in ways that have spawned numerous images of the Indian world that are not entirely accurate." Indeed, characterized in such a fashion not only inaccurate but also "expropriated and utilized on behalf of diverse forms of special pleading" (Steltenkamp, 1983, pp. xii, xv). Ultimately, by allowing Black Elk's life to speak, as the family stories in which his great-great-grandson Maka shared "that much more," then Black Elk's life story "can shed light on the larger, more complex social system within which he lived." And in the process of the unfolding of this book, the discovery of "far more than just one man's life will be better understood" (p. xii).

In addition to those aforementioned, there are others who have encountered Black Elk at some stage in their lives who also have stories to share. Namely, those shared in multiple settings with Black Elk's great-great-[great—details to follow] grandson Maka who, like Black Elk, resides in the Pine Ridge Reservation, growing up with his maternal grandmother Charlotte and grandfather Gerald in what a *RollingStone* reporter described, at the time of Maka's birth in 1987, "a snugly modern house near Manderson" (Greider, 1987, p. 10).

During the year of Maka's birth and interview mentioned, his grandmother Charlotte Black Elk was engaged in preserving the Lakota culture by refining here articulation in both languages Lakota and English and working on sacred texts in written form from stories she had heard as a child. One story in particular, that gives context to Maka's name, was a creation story account regarding the "spirit of Inyan," who is "before anything has meaning," and "beyond understanding." As this story and creation-like story unfolds, Charlotte described the way in which Inyan takes a new form of the earth with the name Maka. And, in this form, Maka in the shape of the earth desired a covering and in this creation of a covering "she calls her children. People of the Four Relations are created: the Growing and Moving Things, the Winged, the Four-Legged, the Two Legged." Charlotte detailed this Native creation story analogous to the Christian creation story in Genesis, where Lakota legends also recollected a "fall from grace," in a process leading to the people calling "themselves the Lakota," as they emerged "from caves in the Black Hills," geographically known to Lakota people as "the heart of everything" (Greider, 1987, pp. 11–12).

Unlike Black Elk, who learned of others informally, at least compared to contemporary perceptions, by way of his immediate Native community, and journeys throughout the Great Plains, including abroad to Europe, Maka was more formally educated contemporarily, as an undergraduate at the University of San Francisco, and then graduate school on the opposite side of the United States at Columbia University. Maka's educational path is exceptional and unique, compared with most enrolled on the Pine Ridge Reservation in South Dakota.

After nearly two years of interviews with Maka, he shared many details regarding his life to date, one of which was formative in terms of his maternal grandparents, who raised and adopted him (thus the great-great and sometimes great reference), and it is why he would call them his parents, who were intentional regarding his K–12 education, primarily for reasons of cultural identity and Lakota tradition, guided by his mother (grandmother), and spiritual, Catholic formation by his father (grandfather). Interestingly, even with the significant influence of years of missionary involvement by Catholic Jesuit priests on the Pine Ridge Reservation, Creighton University in Nebraska as the educational "pipeline" for those few who did go to college, and now more so in recent decades, Maka exercised his independence by breaking emerging trends of attending postsecondary education and Creighton and instead enrolling in another Jesuit institution of higher learning, the University of San Francisco. An independence learned through formation both at home from nurturing, educated parents and the tremendous, exceptional Lakota culture past and present, who holds a familial bond with Black Elk and his cousin Crazy Horse (Personal Communication/Interviews, 2021–2022).

Education has not always been a bright chapter in the exceptional story of the Lakota people, as the colonizing horrors of government and religious-run residential boarding schools mounted in North America. Germane to both Maka and Black Elk, who were neither exposed to such horrors formally, was vicarious exposure, and as current medical professions would stipulate genetically (see more elaborate discussion on trauma ahead), traumatic experiences via stories shared by others. Coupled with both, kept by Black Elk, and currently in keeping with Maka, tremendous responsibility as culture bearers is distinctive and similar, in terms of cognizance of a calling being part of a historically, exceptional Lakota people. And in the shared detrimental impact of such historical trauma, neither were spared the larger ill effects of colonization, which relegated an advanced culture of tens of millions of North American Native people to just below three hundred thousand by 1890, who were forced to live in isolated areas, akin to what some viewed as prisoners of war.

If only such an experience was left in the past for historians to sort out, and emotions to reside only on the pages penned. Yet, the reality is, and it cannot be overstated, millions today, whose roots flow back to the ancestors and contemporaries of Lakota healer Black Elk, suffer under the historical trauma created by centuries of colonization. And while many may aver that the most dramatic examples of such colonization are merely historical, many like Maka, who nobly serve communities that continue to reel from the devastating effects of historical trauma, are enlisting the echoes of leaders such as Black Elk as a way of rediscovering a cultural identity, in the face of past and present attempts to obfuscate such an identity.

Black Elk's Life Speaks: "That Much...More"

The term trauma, in the past and present contexts, has been posited earlier here, and it is prudent to establish some operational, elaborative understanding moving forward to deepen and therefore further the overall intent of this book, which is to consider the way in which Black Elk's life speaks in the face of such trauma as a critical figure modeling cultural healing. In terms of trauma generally, Menakem's (2017) scholarship focused on a physical capacity relative to what always happens "in the body," and that trauma is "not a flaw or a weakness ... not an event." Menakem continued that trauma is a highly effective tool of safety and survival for the

> ... the body's protective response to an event—or series of events—that perceives as potentially dangerous. In the aftermath of highly stressful or traumatic situations, our ... brain may embed a reflexive traumatic response in our brain ... manifest as fight, fight, or freeze ... stuck in the body—and stays there until it is addressed. (p. 7)

The way in which trauma is addressed within the cultural realm today is really at the heart of progress relative to cultural healing, most notably in the United States as healing broadly is viewed as,

> something binary; either we're broken or ... healed ... that's not how healing operates ... it's almost never how human growth works ... healing and [my underline] growth take place on a continuum, with innumerable points between utter brokenness and total health. (Menakem, 2017, p. 12)

And if trauma relative to healing were only defined on these terms, then it would appear manageable, yet as an individual, the impact of trauma is, with the corresponding impact on the collective of culture writ large, neuroscience, and additional work in genetics has uncovered more evidence that trauma is not only impactful due to the way "we treat each other." Rather, it is also transferrable genetically through inheritance, thereby revealing that "trauma can change the expression of the DNA in our cells, and these changes can be passed from parent to child." And while the following evidence of more recent research is emerging, Menakem identified it as "memories connected to painful events ... passed down." Some of these traumatic effects articulated do seem particular to cultural groups such as "prevalent among African Americans, Jews, American Indians, three groups that have experienced an enormous amount of historical trauma" (pp. 39–40).

It would appear the deck is stacked when considering the impact of trauma, historical, and otherwise, in terms of the impacts inhibiting or outright blocking any individual <u>and</u> collective, therapeutic, resilient efforts. Research in the field claims otherwise; in fact, the "effect is not permanent; once the trauma has ceased and been addressed, growth and positive change become possible once again" (Ganguly & Poo, 2013, p. 731).

One more contemporary barrier to progress relative to trauma, which would also be inherent in advancing the premise of this book of Black Elk's life speaking to such progress, is a nuanced version of colonization's weakened, but continued grip held, possibly somewhat surprisingly by "white progressives." Menakem (2017) forwarded an astute recognition of a nuanced disposition exhibited by white progressives, "committed to interventions that ignore or dismiss the crucial role historical trauma plays in people's lives." Not only is this observation astute but also uncanny, and I would stipulate personally and admittingly, was and still can be, all too familiar. Cutting deeper paradoxically, Menakem claimed such interventions in fact "sabotage healing for many Americans of all skin colors, and unwittingly perpetuate the trauma. I hope they will receive these words as a loud wake-up call." Once again, stark news and medicine for some and everyday challenges for others. What is not distinctive, relative to trauma and healing, according to Menakem, in terms of a hopeful, challenging direction, is all of us have bodies that can be impacted by trauma, and

> healing does not occur in a vacuum. We also need to be mending our collective bodies. This mending takes place in connection with our bodies—in groups, neighborhoods, and communities … This communal healing can help us steadily build respect, recognition, communication and, eventually; culture. (p. 132)

As a contribution to this steady build-up to communal and ultimately cultural healing, there is hope indeed, embodied in those with the strongest historical roots, who have a present-day impact, not only on the restoration of cultural identity among Native people but also by seeking an opportunity for cultural healing among all people. In this sense of cultural healing, Black Elk's story, which has been told to many, by many, may need another approach. What is suggested here is his life should speak through his own words, and those related to him, in concert with those who have been about serious, culturally responsive scholasticism as opposed to maybe the more traditional Black Elk canon of voices speaking <u>for</u> his life. In other words, by creating more access points to Black Elk's life, possibly his life can speak to more hearers whatever their plight, in an attempt to perpetuate a more authentic way of recognizing one another in spaces once unfamiliar, and now formed by intercultural affinity (Taylor, 2022).

Modeling in this case, and many others, where this virtuous endeavor is championed, is critical. Ergo, the importance of Black Elk's life speaking to the modeling of a life, navigated both social mores and faith perspectives of other cultures for the benefit of the seminal Lakota saying *Mitákuye Oyás'in*—all are relatives. A life spoken, no doubt, to relatives in a familial lineage defined formally by kinship, bloodline, and beyond. And in the case of bloodline, Black Elk's life can speak in ways exceptional, comparatively at times, when considering accounts beyond this context. A case in point would be Maka's grandparents Charlotte Black Elk and Gerald Clifford who, Black Elk's life had imparted on them, and then imparted on others including Maka, the importance of relationships. As Gerald shared, "to one another as Lakota are defined by our relationships to the earth … Until we get back on track in our relationship to the earth, we cannot straighten out any of our relationships to ourselves, to other people." Charlotte Black Elk expressed a similar familial, prophetic theme shared by her great-grandfather, John Hollow Horn when he danced the outlawed sun dance, "A day will come in your lifetime when the earth, your mother, will be you, with tears running, to save her. Ho, if you fail to help her, you [Lakota] and all people will die like dogs. Remember this" (Greider, 1987, pp. 15–16).

Black Elk's story is remarkable on a number of levels and inspires me, a non-Native, as I step into more and more cultural spaces and find an affinity for those I was once separated from for decades, when I lived the urban, suburban, and then rural life attributed to "White flight" from culturally diversifying communities. Black Elk's start in life was not unlike others during his time or even today. Visiting his birthplace "…along the banks of the Little Powder River, [where] White Cross Sees [gave] birth to a baby boy named Kahnigapi ("Choice")," I couldn't help but ponder my own birth in Pontiac, Michigan, to Rod and Phyllis Taylor, who were quite advanced in age as they brought two families together during the tumult of the mid-1960s. As Black Elk matured in his younger years, his baby boy Lakota's name evolved, as so many did, into his father's, Hehaka Sapa (Black Elk), a medicine man and cousin of the famed warrior and visionary, Crazy Horse. With these roots and family stories forming Black Elk, was also a sense of belonging to the Oglala, one of seven bands of the Lakota, and "the name … now ran through four generations" (Oldmeadow, 2018, p. 33).

While most of Black Elk's people would have lived within a vast radius encompassing what presently is the Montana, Wyoming, and North and South Dakota border areas prior to and during European contact, Black Elk's life transcended this, given radius in extraordinary ways, all things considered. The colonizing pressure, exerted by a growing White American presence stretching from the east coast to the Great

Plains, troubled and displaced Black Elk's family, among many other Native American people. While he did stay as rooted with his people as much as would be expected, he did venture to other lands a few short years following his adolescence, including Europe. Stories abound regarding his exploits, like the following:

> When the queen [Victoria] departed, her subjects bowed in honor to her, but she bowed to the assembled Indians …. Unable to speak English, they wandered around London until they were arrested by police as possible suspects in a crime that would later be associated with Jack the Ripper. An interpreter verified that they were not involved in the incident and suggested they connect with a smaller show that was comparable to Buffalo Bill's. (Steltenkamp, 2009, pp. 55–56)

Travels abroad are only a fraction of this seminal Native healer's life, which included events such as the Battle of Little Big Horn, travels with Sitting Bull, and many others, to Canada and back, and the horrors of the Massacre at Wounded Knee. It is no surprise that many wonder about life such as Black Elk's, and subsequent meaning, that began with participation in a thriving Native exceptional Lakota culture, experienced travels to Europe, and suffered seeing his people on the verge of a total holocaust. DeMallie (1984) aptly drew attention to the salient question that this book hopefully can bring to the surface: "How was it that a nineteenth-century Lakota mystic could live a full half of the twentieth century on the Pine Ridge Reservation in harmony with the encroaching white man's world?" (p. xxii).

The remaining of this book is an attempt to understand more fully DeMallie's (1984) query by exploring this period of time and the way in which Black Elk's life speaks through the lens of stories. A critical component of the stories threading through this book is a contemporary view offered by a family member who has heard these stories passed down, namely Black Elk's great-great-great grandson Maka. **First**, this book will examine the context of stories prior to and during European contact, focusing first on Black Elk and his people as exceptional people, then an exploration of the impact of European contact fueled by the Doctrine of Discovery. **Second**, the book will zero in on representations with the theme of stories related to the Doctrine of Discovery specifically embodied in missionaries, and the impact their anthropology had on Native people such as Black Elk. **Third**, with this contextual backdrop established, the stories of Black Elk's descendants will be featured to reinforce and deepen such stories alluded to early in the book. **Fourth**, the theme of stories will continue in a summative and concluding fashion, with consideration of the implications of Black Elk's life speaking today and into the future as a mystical beacon for cultural healing, amid the ever-present challenges associated with trauma and survivance.

CHAPTER 1

Stories of Exceptionality and Discovery

Everett Collection/Shutterstock.com

I n an attempt to discern just how stories from a variety of sources may contribute to appreciating how Black Elk's life speaks, first and foremost a step back to the essence of Black Elk's people is important to understand just who the Lakota people were prior to European contact and colonization.

STORIES OF EXCEPTIONAL PEOPLE

Both interviews with Maka and background research seem to affirm that prior to European contact (as Maka would say prevails today), the Lakota people self-identify as exceptional. This is in part due to the legacy of leadership demonstrated by people like Black Elk and others, not necessarily as skills exhibited by only a few Lakota but as the behavior of all members together successfully overcoming the challenges of the Great Plains. As Maka shared,

Sections from Abstract 1, *Black Elk's Life Speaks: "That Much...More" by Michael W. Taylor. Presented at the Fourteenth Biennial Native American Symposium, Abstract 1* at Southeastern Oklahoma State University on November 12, 2021. Reprinted by permission of Michael W. Taylor and Southeastern Oklahoma State University, Native American Symposium.

1

Lakota people … are a community that's just inclined to really accept that they're exceptional people. That was just embedded culturally, it was the case that for Lakota people, the way our society worked pre-European contact was that … We have these different words for leadership and for these different positions in leadership. And we have all these senses of different protocols and ways that leaders behaved and where this whole … You have to know the culture to understand that, but there's a real sense that life on the Great Plains … Especially pre-horse culture, but even after horse culture because horses didn't come until the 1500s, was incredibly difficult. And survival was really … perilous; it was a very difficult thing. (Personal communication/interview, 2021–2022)

In a familial sense, the grounding of Maka's shared thoughts echo, in terms of exceptionality, from his maternal grandmother or as Maka would identify as a mother due to adoption, who expressed, "she was raised for this moment in history … 100 years in the making," while growing up in the same area of Pine Ridge as Maka, "in a canyon settlement … a pocket of resistance where the clan of Crazy Horse settle after the Indian wars … still taught to speak Lakota and told the stories of the old faith." Charlotte Black Elk gave further evidence as she "listened and remembered" to stories focused on this pocket of resistance as an example within this section of stories of exceptional people, by sharing the foundational legacy of "long-ago grandfathers including holy men and distinguished rebels— Hollow Horn, Plenty Wolf, Sun Dreamer, Black Elk." She pointed to Hollow Horn as an exemplar of resistance as he "performed a sun dance at Manderson in 1929 in defiance of the Indian agency" (Greider, 1987, pp. 9–11).

Charlotte Black Elk emphasized the importance of the complex organization by elders as "Those Who Speak of Sacred Things kept the secrets alive." And in doing so organizationally, she said, "people knew exactly what they were doing. The elders taught us to get an education and learn to speak English better than the white people because, they said, 'Someday you're going to fight this battle.'" The resurrection of this exceptionality while similar historically also was, and some may view as, still distinctive. Charlotte Black Elk shared that elders were very cognizant of a lost generation "to the civilizers and the Christian … to traumatic change and alcohol." With the force of resonance heard throughout interviews with Charlotte's grandson Maka, and walking with many Native people within, and beyond the confines of formal higher education, it would seem evident to me the responsibility of this newer ascendancy of exceptionality may be finite in nature, with final hope resting in a generation. A generation Charlotte identified as one that "would be the last—if we did not fight the battle—because the others would go the way of drugs or choose not to be Lakota. This was the obligation placed on the grandchildren" (Greider, 1987, pp. 9–11).

While the exceptionality of the Lakota people at the time prior to European contact was characterized by unified perseverance in the face of the grit of Plains life, it was also grounded in a faith perspective predicated on a belief "… that what the Creator had given us was enough and that the place he had put us was where we belonged. We wanted to learn the Creator's original teachings in the land that he had given us. We were an honoring people, a guardian people …" (Nerburn, 2009, p. 299). Herein is where discord may have come at the hands of contact, as European ideas pervaded the ancestral lands where the Lakota people had lived for centuries because those who eventually came for colonizing purposes would never quite be satisfied with enough, whether it be purely material or spiritual. Despite this discord and history, as the truth-teller who ended up on the dominant side of the discord, the exceptional nature of the Lakota people is what Frazier (2000) identified, noting, "a surprising amount of Oglala [Lakota] culture is the same today as it was in pre-reservation times … [it] still produce[s] heroes, despite the fact that the wide market for them seems to have waned … they have always honored warriors; and … children as well" (p. 19).

When attempting to defend a country or people rendered nearly defenseless by the hands of colonialism, ties to the land that bred such an exceptional people is what some scholars of Native spirituality would link to a mystical attitude

> toward the world … both practical and mythopoetic in their relations with nature. They knew the environment in impressive details … and … know the world as a connective unit whose parts—including themselves—existed only in relation to each other as a whole … All entities in the Indian worldview were potentially equivalent … American Indians depended on nature for survival, and in recognizing their dependence, they expressed a range of emotions from hope, complaint, and remorse, to fear … as expressed in prayers and offerings. (Vecsey & Venables, 1980, pp. 16–17)

Consequently, it was within this legacy of exceptionality, in connection to both the land and one another both physically and spiritually, that Black Elk was situated "to adapt to new circumstances and situations. The nomadic life gave the Lakota people a willingness to negotiate many changes of environment and place … [T]hese qualities … found their source, strength and resilience in the way they lived with the supernatural" (Archambault, 1998, pp. 25–26). Maka put it succinctly, complementing a sense of the supernatural with the practical:

> You had to place profound trust in leaders who show that they were smart enough, capable enough, made the right decisions, and who were humble enough. These are all the characteristics that show up into the Lakota values, that are important ... And still to this day because of ... Lakota culture, even pre-contact until now. We value people who step up and step forward and who show themselves being incredible leaders. And that's why we have all these significant names, Crazy Horse, Sitting Bull, Black Elk, American Horse, all these people who at some point in their lives, demonstrated profound ability to lead. Black Elk has that status in the community and has had it for a while, where people find Black Elk to be fascinating. (Personal communication/interview, 2021–2022)

As a good summary of this portion of the book, Steltenkamp (1993) approaches Maka's sense of the exceptional prior to and in anticipation of European contact. He also pointed to adaptation, noting that what some may try to fix historically

> ... was in fact still forming or evolving for this non-static Plains culture ... [T]heir continued survival was as contingent upcoming a relationship with the Sacred as it was upon the forces they faced in everyday profane life ... [which] becomes transparent only after a careful scrutiny of persons such as Black Elk whose generation strove to pass on this legacy. (p. 15)

STORIES OF DISCOVERY

Though stories of an exceptional Lakota legacy persisted for centuries in and around the Great Plains of North America, different stories of discovery were persisting on a broader scope from Europe, passing on a legacy often in contrast and eventually in direct conflict with the Lakota way of life. The blueprint for this story of discovery was the Doctrine of Discovery (DOD), which according to Charles and Rah (2019) emerged from a series of fifteenth-century official decrees, or papal bulls, by Pope Nicholas V that essentially granted permission

> to King Alfonso V of Portugal "to invade, search out, vanquish, and subdue all Saracens (Muslims) and pagans ... and other

enemies of Christ wheresoever placed ... and to *reduce their persons to perpetual slavery,* and to apply and appropriate to himself and to all successors the kingdoms ... possessions, and goods, and to convert them to his and their use and profit. (p. 15)

As the DODs expanded to North America, indigenous people first welcomed that intent on not only discovery but also initially to what assimilation of culture to the only culture ordained by such a doctrine proclaimed. And while those indigenous may have been welcoming at first, as John Neihardt's daughter Hilda Neihardt (1995) observed,

> ... It [became] all strange and wrong to the invaded ones, but they could not stop the oncoming flood of whites, however bravely they fought against it. And so, as people do when faced with seemingly insurmountable difficulty, they turned to dreams and the hope of spiritual intervention .... (pp. 9–10)

In the attempt to access the spiritual realm for help against the strangers, the Lakota people, like other indigenous peoples, turned to divine intervention via sacred rituals like a dance. As Hilda Neihardt (1995) also pointed out, from initial contact to what most recognize as the time of the near-cataclysmic end of Native people,

> Because most white people did not understand the meaning of all that dancing, which seemed foolish to them, it was called the "Ghost Dance craze." Thinking the nearly destitute, unarmed Indians were preparing for war, they called on the army for protection—*protection from dancing*! As history records, this vision of inspired hope of the Plains tribes ended tragically in the bloody snow of the Wounded Knee massacre on December 29, 1890. This happening would mark the end of organized Indian resistance on the plains. (pp. 9–10)

"Where is the shame, the outrage, or even a day in court?" Some may ask this question when they become cognizant of such tragic events. With regard to legal considerations, there would appear to be ways in which those establishing a hold on the land with doctrine in hand may argue or have argued both ends of this case. Charles and Soong-Chan (2019) touched on cases in which Native communities were identified as "foreign entities" in terms of their relationship with the US Government. For example, an 1831 ruling concerning the *Cherokee Nation v. Georgia* stipulated "that Native tribes were 'domestic dependent nations' existing 'in a state of pupilage. Their relation to the United States resembles that of a ward to his guardian'" (p. 103).

In this lies the struggle even today when considering treaties such as the Fort Laramie Treaty and thousands of acres like the Black Hills and Powder River areas sacred to the Lakota and neighboring indigenous peoples. Whereas it appears that treaties are binding with foreign entities, legal wordsmithing presently translates Indian tribes as wards in relation to the US Government, and arguments for land retrieval seem to go mute, although recent developments among Native people in areas like Oklahoma may show a crack in such legal contortion. Overall, as Charles and Soong-Chan (2019) so fittingly opined,

> When you are in possession of stolen property, and the people you stole it from are right in front of you, the only just thing to do is give it back. Whether you are attempting to hoard it or to share it is irrelevant. Both actions are unjust. White Americans are not superior to anybody. Turtle Island is not Europe's promised land. And you cannot discover lands that are already inhabited. (p. 131)

An inhabited claim was preserved, even in the wake of near-genocidal destruction of Native people at large and Lakota people in particular, during Black Elk's life span until 1950 and beyond. For example, Black Elk's descendant, Charlotte and husband Clifford, Maka's grandparents, engaged in the legal struggle with many others, who were also faced at times historically with an impossible "sell or starve" choice relative to the forced relegation to reservations and the forced relinquishment of sacred lands such as the Black Hills. Whereas in the late 1800s, such measures, including the banning of indigenous religious practices due to government agents perceiving such practices as "resistance" to non-Native occupation of such lands, these measures, and more left Lakota at that time as "broken as a people." A testimony to the resiliency and exceptionality of people perceived as "broken" became a misnomer since near genocide, at the close of the 1800s, nearly one hundred years later when after several landmark legal battles. For example, legal battles over mineral-rich lands like the Black Hills finally resulted in the "largest Indian-claims settlement ever awarded," which in today's dollars equates to about 2.5 billion dollars. While a substantial sum indeed, "the Black Hills mines alone yielded more than $2 billion in gold, not to mention uranium and other ores." Legally, matters such as these and others have been wrangled throughout the court system as significant as the U.S. Supreme Court (Greider, 1987, pp. 8–9).

And even with victory in court relative to the aforementioned monetary award, the primary goal of the Lakota people was "the return of the Black Hills." So, therefore, all "eight tribal councils passed resolutions refusing the settlement of their claim, demanding the land instead." Survivance is on full display here, by exceptional people, who see the forest through the trees in terms of knowing someday their active resistance and engagement instead of victimhood, will persevere despite even today as,

> lawyers on the case still shuffle papers and appear in court. The Lakota still will not accept the award. The money still accumulates interest in the Treasury Department. And *Sioux Nation of Indians v. University States of America* languishes in a legal limbo, a living monument to the mysteries of the white man's law. (Greider, 1987, pp. 8–9)

The superiority abounding in this story of discovery seems to be shared by a number of institutions, secular and religious alike—as such domination of people, like Black Elk's Lakota people, may not have been possible without collusion among such institutions. As hard as it may be to read the DOD relative to the eventual establishment of the United States, along with Christian churches solidifying the superiority of a superior God over Native traditions, it is a story Maka called "complicated" because it is a story

> full of a lot of pain, in terms of even just how Christianity came to this country. I belong to a group that is writing ... the next pastoral plan for Native ministry. So they've got a number of people on, including myself, who are writing these different sections that will eventually come together. And the bishops will, hopefully ... approve it. And the section that I'm working on, that I was having dialogue within this group, was about that history and about how we have a very delicate responsibility.... (Personal communication/interview, 2021–2022)

The delicacy in terms of responsibility, past and present, referring to Maka's involvement with the U.S. Catholic Bishops is understandable. Yet also considered is the decades of frustration expressed by those before Maka, and today by those who express hope yet concern that some rhetoric may be more echoes of the Doctrine of the Discovery, and the wreckage in its wake. Maka expressed such hope yet, tangentially, frustration in this process of acknowledgment and possible action relative to the DOD, as Christian churches and, in particular, the Catholic

Church through its process of drafting various documents somewhat related to this doctrine,

> When it comes to this idea of the continual encountering and conversion toward the Gospel, that that's the thing every culture is called to do. And that every culture can do, and it's not about replacing or changing that culture, it's about perfecting and deepening a relationship to God in any culture. That doesn't have to change who we are. That's often a narrative that's imposed on other communities. We never seriously sit down and say, "Does white America still like to keep doing that? Or do they do that already? Did they figure it out?" What does the non-indigenous community in this country, in this Catholic Church, what is their continued call to conversion? And how is that rooted in recognizing how they didn't do that historically, in the way in which they first encountered indigenous peoples? (Personal communication/interview, 2021–2022)

So, it would appear with historical revelations abounding regarding the ills of the DOD, within Christian churches like the Catholic Church, hierarchal wheels may need to move more promptly, which runs counter to centuries of pragmatism in the face of cultural winds. However, when considering those members of such churches whose ancestors and selves are still under the oppressive thumb of the DOD, it is as Maka said in his own draft for the U.S. Bishops that such bureaucracy

> really gets in the way because according to the bishops I've spoken with about Doctrine of Discovery, they'll say, "It was rescinded in 15 something." Or they'll point ... to a different papal bull, [that] talks about how indigenous people of the Americas have souls ... And I think it was 30 some years after the initial Doctrine of Discovery papal bull. And so they'll always be like, "Well, that's when it was repealed. That's when the pope then said "nope, that was wrong." (Personal communication/ interview, 2021–2022)

And as the interview continued along the lines of the DOD and the culpability of Christian churches, especially the Catholic Church, it would appear there is further rationalization of what history's ills are and what distinguishes today's disposition regarding such history. For example, Maka shared that the oft-used reference to the Catholic Church's distancing itself from the DOD centuries prior is a "Catholic cop-out." He went on to share that the Church's apparent distancing from the ill effects of the DOD may be suspect precisely because of its lack of effect:

> to anyone, especially on the side of the indigenous community, or the communities of color in general across the Americas will say, "Okay. [The follow-up papal bull], did that change anything?"… Colonization, horrific violent colonization continued, even after you said that we have souls. Whoop dee doo! It's Catholic doctrine, so the adherence to it and the academic dimension, that says "well this idea changed during this [new] papal bull here." The bishops need to recognize that that isn't good enough. That pointing out that it was a period a long time ago, in a different papal bull, isn't good enough because it didn't change behavior. (Personal communication/ interview date, 2021–2022)

More recent events, in the summer of 2022, regarding Pope Francis's visit to offer a formal apology to the Indigenous Peoples in Canada, may alter the course of centuries for the Catholic Church in relation to Native people, and time will tell no doubt as it has over the centuries of colonization. This could be the moment of a significant shift, and as the author of this book, I would be remiss without including Pope Francis's words shared in what might be historically exceptional and significant when compared with any other efforts attempted by the Catholic Church.

In the Pope's visit, identified as a "penitential pilgrimage … asking forgiveness," he used unmistakably clear language focusing on how it is "necessary to remember how the policies of assimilation and enfranchisement, which also included the residential school system, were devastating for the people of these lands." The Pope continued with the potential of "great opportunity among European colonists when first arriving to bring about "fruitful encounter between cultures, traditions, and forms of spirituality." Furthermore, with histories' tremendous wake of colonial destruction of any such potential, Pope Francis accounted for that history strikingly through stories

> you told [Indigenous people told]: how the policies of assimilation ended up systematically marginalizing the indigenous people … I thank you for making me appreciate this, for telling me about the heavy burdens that you still bear, for sharing with me these bitter memories. (*America*, 2022, pp. 1–7)

And while the Pope noted that Christian charity was not completely absent during this time,

> the overall effects of policies ... were catastrophic. What our Christian faith tells us is that this was a disastrous error, incompatible with the Gospel of Jesus Christ ... In the face of this deplorable evil, the Church kneels before God and implores his forgiveness for the sins of her children (Pope John Paul II, *Incarnationis Mysterium*) ... I humbly beg forgiveness for the evil committed by so many Christians against the indigenous people. (*America*, 2022, pp. 1–7)

And finally, Pope Francis on the front end of his several days' tour of atonement in Canada set the tone for the balance of the tour and future in terms of stripping the cloak of the DOD, though never formally mentioning it at this stage,

> Our efforts are not enough to achieve healing and reconciliation: we need God's grace. We need the quiet and powerful wisdom of the Spirit, the tender love of the Comforter. May he bring to fulfillment the deepest expectations of our hearts. May he guide our steps and enable us to advance together on our journey. (*America*, 2022, pp. 1–7)

Even in the wake of Pope Francis's hope-filled Canadian visit, as newer potential evidence offered to reconcile the trauma-infused effects of the DOD, time will indeed tell. Tell, in terms of whether stories of discovery will fade formally with the pieces of historical trauma left to acknowledge and support tangibly culturally responsive reparations in terms of mental, spiritual, and overall cultural healing. In addition, the jaded legacy of stories of discovery, though historically situated for the purposes of this book, establishes a context for Black Elk's life speaking from his life's beginning at the confluence of the Powder and Little Powder Rivers to his gravesite in Manderson on the current Pine Ridge Reservation. It would appear such stories persist within the complexity that Maka lamented during his 2021–2022 interviews. Sweeney (2021) called this story of discovery the colonialism of Christianity, an aspect of colonialism that has become "...the normative explanation for how Christianity functioned in the life of the Oglala and every other tribe of Native people ... But we have such a hard time seeing... Black Elk for who he was if we cannot see beyond the mold of this common understanding" (p. 57). A key point highlighted by Sweeney regarding "seeing" Black Elk is beyond this normative sense of the colonialism of Christianity.

Herein is the challenge of Black Elk's life speaking past, present, and future. Stories like discovery and doctrines such as the DOD must be fully realized by those often immune from the historical trauma such readings inflict. And, paradoxically, by those whose recognition is critical for a reciprocal sense of cultural healing to occur, within the context of stories such as Black Elk's. Subsequent stories that are fully represented and critical as a model of such healing, in the spirit of healing, as more stories and understandings must be shared, particularly those that bring into relief Sweeney's sense of the colonialism of Christianity.

CHAPTER 2

Stories of the Colonization of Christianity, Anthropology, and Missionaries

Sergey Kohl/Shutterstock.com

olonization, in general, is as dated in centuries prior to such complexities as the colonization of Christianity. Nevertheless, for the purposes of this book, such colonization typified Black Elk's formative years, as Enochs (1996) pointed out: "In the 1870's and 1880's, the government divided the Sioux bands and restricted them to different reservations in the Dakota Territory. This undermined their national unity and obstructed their ability to hold their traditional national councils" (p. 85).

Regarding this undermining of tradition among individual tribes and inter-tribal relations by colonial efforts of both Christians and governments, Dussias (1997) argued that Native Americans are no longer subjected to such obstruction overtly like their "nineteenth-century ancestors," because there still does seem to be a skepticism "over whether their beliefs and practices are religious in nature, [presenting] difficulties in making their beliefs and practices comprehensible in non-Indians, and the privileges of property rights and other interests over their free exercise rights." Further, Dussais acknowledged that though the government's Christianization policy, which featured "overt suppression of traditional Native American religious practices," is not what it once was, still today, "freedom to practice their religion remains illusory for many Native Americans" (p. 851).

Though not as overtly intense, this sense of suppression of traditional Native American religious practice remains, despite the efforts of recent historical figures, Pope Francis's recent aforementioned "penitential pilgrimage" to Canada, and some saints in the Catholic Church such as Pope John Paul II, who consistently advocated both in speech in and church documents for "the dignity and rights of the native people of the Americas by insisting that they not be deprived of their freedom or the possession of their property" (as cited in Archambault et al., 2003, p. 155).

Pope John Paul II pushed even further during a Pontifical Council for Cultures, issuing explicit instructions for the Catholic Church's contact with cultures by stating that the Church "must welcome all that is compatible with the Gospel in these traditions of the peoples, in order to bring the richness of Christ ... [and] to be enriched herself by the manifold wisdom of the nations of the earth" (Archambault et al., 2003, p. 223). With a sense of tenuous momentum garnered, from as significant a pope in Catholic Church history as Pope John Paul II, the US Catholic Bishops affirmed and challenged Native American Catholics by affirming the Pope's call

> To ... keep alive your cultures, your languages, the values and customs which have served you well in the past and which provide a solid foundation for the future. Your encounter with the Gospel has not only enriched you; it has enriched the Church. We are well aware that this has not taken place without its difficulties and occasionally, its blunders. However,... the Gospel does not destroy what is best in you ... it enriches the spiritual qualities and gifts that are distinctive of your cultures ... Here I wish to urge the local churches to be truly "catholic" in their outreaches to Native peoples and to show respect and honor for their culture and all their worthy traditions ... All consciences must be challenged. There are real injustices to be addressed and biased attitudes to be challenged. (pp. 226–227)

Similar to the explicit language shared previously by Pope Francis and his historical visit to Canada to atone for the colonial sins of the Catholic Church, it is hard to mistake the explicit language of the Catholic Church via one of its seminal popes like John Paul II. Most noteworthy is the urge to be truly catholic, almost echoing those missionaries' centuries prior such as the Jesuits, who through their command of language and learning, without blemish, bridged cultural divides and faith perspectives, which is ultimately what drew key Lakota leaders such as Red Cloud and Black Elk into a constructive relationship with Christianity via the Catholic Church.

Yet, still recalling Dussias's (1997) hopeful and sobering thoughts expressed earlier regarding overt oppressive barriers to traditional faith perspectives such as those held by "nineteenth-century ancestors," there is this underlying "skepticism" regarding such Native faith perspectives religious in nature that are embodied in their beliefs and practices. Though Dussias's apt analysis does identify a lingering challenge, in terms of cultural understanding and the pervading skepticism aforementioned, there is also implied hope. Hope not only in the fact that outright brutal oppression to the point of genocide does not exist today in the United States but also more pointedly back to the intent of this book and the ability for a cultural, iconic symbol in the person of Black Elk's life, given the fully realized ability to speak. As Costello (2005) captured well to this end,

> Even today Black Elk's vision has a message that needs to be heard ... [he] teaches us that the problem of Western expansion was not in bringing the gospel to the Lakota; instead ... was not hearing the gospel. The focus on nonviolence, equality, and the rejection of greed—the firm rejection of colonialism—is the witness that Black Elk's vision preached and still preaches to Western Christianity, to the church, and to the broken world. Despite the tragedy of Western colonialism, there is still hope, there is still time to hear and respond to the gospel. Black Elk, a great saint of the colonial era, still calls all people through his vision and the witness of his life to hear the Lakota Christ; colonialism must end so the sacred tree may one day bloom for all people. (p. 182)

In order to discern further both the skepticism and hope, as a result of Western colonialism, it may be helpful to turn to the academy and those who were charged with understanding Native people during the past few centuries of colonialism and Christianity. Though still emerging as a field of study in terms of human cultural anthropology, not fully developing until the 1900s, academics were sent to the field to understand Native people as they wrestled with the rapidly unfolding traumatic events. In many senses, it was this emerging academic discipline that helped establish the sense of skepticism today, despite what we know today more accurately of research and stories of Native spiritual tradition and custom.

STORIES OF ANTHROPOLOGY

Anthropology is a broad field, but its practitioners provoked strikingly surgical colonizing implications most notably in the area of Native spiritual practice.

Even though most in the academy, during the initial exploration of Native culture centuries past, were aware of the multiplicity of tribes throughout North America, this sense of diversity seemed to abate when considering spiritual practice. Realization of such a phenomenon was affirmed during the interview with Maka, who had made reference to a "misnomer," because of the varied spiritual beliefs, traditions, and practices exhibited by "hundreds of tribes." Overall, Maka described "early anthropologists" as

> trying to categorize and make sense of the Native American spirituality, Shamanism and Animism was the main categorical marker. But that really creates a false picture of what, certainly to some Lakota people, what they believe. Because with Shamanism, they describe it like you worship the medicine man or you worship the sky, this human being who you believe is holy figure. And that's what our religion was initially classified as, was Shamanism, an Animistic Shamanism. (Personal communication/interview, 2021–2022)

In hindsight, if 20/20 may lead some to speculate when judging the errors of the academy's past, yet even a cursory review of relations among both religious and/or academic bodies can see some lingering effects of perceptions of animistic shamanism. Even following Neihardt's (1932/1971) seminal work *Black Elk Speaks,* and Joseph Epes Brown (1971), who also had direct contact with Black Elk a few years prior to his death confessed, "...almost all he said was phrased in terms of involving animals and natural phenomena. I naively wished that he would begin to talk about religious matters, until I finally realized he was, in fact, explaining his religion" (as cited in Vecsey & Venables, 1980, p. 1). And while some still were convinced of some kind of pagan roots of Native spiritual practice, similar to Epes Brown's realization, others came to see what Maka described as "illuminating" in terms of what Native people like the Lakota believed in "one God, one Creator, one Spirit." In fact, he went on further to share as a family descendant that when "Black Elk himself talk about how this idea [one God, Creator, Spirit]... there's a center and that that center is the Creator. And that part of our job is to recognize that that center is in each of us and is everywhere" (Personal communication/interview, 2021–2022).

The complexity of Native spirituality and historic misinterpretation from disciplines like anthropology and even additional emissaries of colonization like missionaries, who may have not perceived this sense of animistic shamanism; still misrepresentation pervaded with other layers of complexity existed that often added clues and insights. For example, the complexity around the symbol of the

Trickster, which was not static in interpretation internally culturally, let alone externally. According to Radin (1972), the Trickster was another clue into the insight of Native spirituality; paradoxically, "no generation understands him fully, but no generation can do without him," as he helps to personify the differentiation of "god and man ... present within every individual" (pp. 168–169). Often this paradoxical, symbolic approach via such a Trickster figure was one of the other ways that Brown (1971) observed that

> The Indian actually identifies ... with, or becomes, the quality or principle of the being or thing which comes ... in a vision ... In order that this 'power may never leave ... always carries ... some material form representing the ... object from which ... [he] received ... "power." These objects have often been incorrectly called fetishes, whereas they actually correspond more precisely to what the Christian calls guardian angels, since for the Indian, the animals and birds, and all things, are the "reflections"—in a material form—of the Divine principles. (p. 45)

Complexities abounding within Native spirituality, and their parallels with the Christianity of those viewing Native people historically anthropologically and otherwise, seem to have some areas that may be far from an intersection or even reconciliation, according to seminal Lakota healer Black Elk, who DeMallie (1984) said, refused to accept a troubling view expressed by missionaries "that the Lakota religion was evil, the work of the devil ..." And although Black Elk seems to have accepted Christianity, "he nonetheless still believed that the Lakota religion was good and true and that there was something in it of value not only to the Lakotas, but to all mankind" (p. 93).

Whether deemed evil, pagan, shamanistic, or animistic, continued words of encouragement appear at times through cracks in a wall of perception layered by centuries of misperception. One representative thought comes in dialogue and correspondence with Milwaukee Archbishop Rembert G. Weakland and Native Americans:

> Their spirituality was called pagan; the boarding schools served to weaken the social system which might have served to sustain many individuals. The Church looks upon the Indian more positively now. One priest ... called their old religion the purest form of religion. (as cited in Archambault et al., 2003, pp. 193–194)

Again, while these various evolving thoughts about Native spirituality are encouraging, what is required is more dialogue with Native people in general, and Native scholars in particular. Oldmeadow (2018) aptly pointed to the difficulty for those who view Native tradition from the outside, or the "educated mind," "to understand their preoccupation … with all things of the Universe, as shown in their myths and hundreds of songs … every created object is important simply because they know the metaphysical correspondence between this world and the real..."—a preoccupation that Black Elk saw as a significant, spiritual understanding within all of us (p. 150).

Within the context of the myth mentioned, Thiel and Vecsey (2012) drew attention to the reinterpretation of tradition as an approach to "an understanding of ethnic identity through the myths of people use to define who they are, where they come from, and the meaning of life." The authors enlisted Preston's work regarding the nature of myths as "corporate not private dreams, pointing toward realities intuitively encountered by human communities, realities conceived to be beyond ordinary experience." Preston also pointed out that myths do "practical things" in terms of the classification of plans and animals and "define appropriate and in appropriate social relations such as kinship rules and legitimize power structures." One other notable myth function opined by Preston is as "healing fictions," stimulating cures through rituals centered on key values in collective religious experience (as cited in Thiel & Vecsey, 2012, p. 105).

Overall, Thiel and Vecsey (2012) pointed to the critical importance of myth and myth-making for Native people, that is, Mohawk, as they "seek to rediscover their identity, struggle for legitimate authority, and seek ways to be healed through a return to myth origins." A process of rediscovery, by the way, is not reserved for Native people alone, but in concert with other religious imaginative traditions, according to the authors, like Catholicism that consists of an expression of ritual through a "variety of avenues." All in all, "these ritual activities tie individuals back into what their culture defines as 'sacred,' resolving alienation and revitalizing a sense of community solidarity," which could be argued interculturally and for the benefit of cultural healing at large (p. 105).

In terms of Black Elk specifically, Brown (2001) said that he was speaking a language that was sacred and metaphysical and grounded in the living realities, "in the immediacy of one's experience." Often this experience was modeled by Black Elk himself who "could describe his religious experience in this manner because he … did not dichotomize human and animal, nature and supernatural." And in this example often modeled by Black Elk, the typical Western distinctions between animism and animatism made it difficult to validate as present to the Native

American experiences since all forms and aspects of creation are experienced as living and animate …" As Brown continued with his analysis supported by "abundant recorded materials," it seemed to affirm a Supreme Being "common among most, if not all, Native American peoples well before the coming of white people and Christian missionaries" (Brown, 2001, pp. 83–84).

One constant, well before the coming of others in contact with Native people, has been the nature of language in relation to cultural identity, as Vecsey (1991) poignantly described: Native beliefs "are encased in, and manifested through, linguistic structures that are … foreign to English-speakers … always exist for non-Indians in translation, through filters." Vecsey also points out that while accessibility is available throughout time, the discernment of Native beliefs, "like all religions … are historically permutable." With this shifting sense of change over history, confronting the challenges of colonization, for example, Native people have attempted to "discover 'access points'… to the sacred that are often impossible to know before the dreams or visions that reveal them." Despite this, Vecsey cautioned, where control is properly ordered in terms of underlying regularities concerning where such access points to the sacred are most located in space and time and where entry into the sacred is most common (although not guaranteed), "the ultimate control of this process is in the hands of the spirits, who must decide if the supplicant or petitioners are worthy of admission to the sacred" (p. 104). This notion of space and time is supported by Jackson (2016) who referred to the "*wasichu* God" as the god of time who acted in history and would come to judge the righteous and unrighteous, the quick and the dead, and the Indian God as the god of space, not time. "Whereas the white God called people forward to a future kingdom, the Indian God was ever-present, in the plains and lakes, not so much imminent as always there" (p. 287).

The intricate nature of this spiritual devotion, when discerned, can provide perspective. Brown (2001) pointed to less inclined discernment, in terms of the romantic, superficial nature in which Native religious traditions are depicted. Black Elk once again surfaces as an exemplar who can, as he did for Brown, explode "romantic [ideas] about these manners …" As Brown came to understand, the close relationship between the human and the natural that is shaped by sacred values has a helpful pragmatic dimension, assisting with the perception of the "complexity behind romantic stereotypes, can help us all understand that a respectful, sacred relationship with the natural world can still be sustaining" (p. 86).

A similar reflection was shared by Maka, who said this was Black Elk "expressing what is a very complex view of God." Further, Maka opined, Christians at the time lacked a full sense of this view expressed by Black Elk. Despite this historic deficiency, Maka hopefully, yet pragmatically said,

> We're getting there today, a bit better. But he's talking about this singular force, this singular creator, that is at the same time this one entity. But that is also, at the same time, in all of us and everywhere and in everything ... Releasing in all those creations, that universality of a creator. That to me is something that he understood. I think he even understood that Catholics at the time probably didn't fully get that. And he was trying, in his own way, to enrich the Catholic faith with what he was relating to it. (Personal communication/interview, 2021–2022)

The complexity here yet the simplicity in which Maka articulates here as getting better—even "a bit better." And when considering Maka's own formation, particularly from his (grand) parents, namely Clifford, who was formed differently from his wife Charlotte, in the Catholic Church nearly becoming a priest with the support of his mother, regardless of different spiritual paths, both were seeking their authentic identity as Lakota people by stripping off layers of assimilation with the question: "What does it mean to be an Indian?" And while Charlotte's and Clifford's cultural experiences were varied, both imparted a sense of convergence to their (grand) son. For Clifford, this sense of convergence developed slowly "between Catholic and Lakota faiths in the figure of Jesus." Historically, Clifford added to this convergence with stories he had heard from his own familial lineage "descended from an interpreter for Chief Red Cloud who married into the tribe," that when missionaries arrived, "Lakotas were very impressed with Jesus ... They thought Jesus was a very good Lakota. He fasted on a mountaintop ... talked to the winds and the birds ... did the ultimate thing—dying so the people would live" (Greider, 1987, pp. 12–13).

Today, the convergence of spiritual perspectives may be more amenable to more people in a slow and deliberate process highlighted by both Maka, and in the experiences of his grandfather Clifford, and great, great, great-grandfather Black Elk. Of course, the navigation of such experiences, somewhat reminiscent of the past, is not without challenges in terms of opportunities for convergence between Native spirituality and Christianity. This opportunity for convergence in general was most likely a result of his Oglala cultural heritage, which Sweeney (2021) offers as "centered around many ideas and practices wise and valuable." Sweeney commented further that these earth-honoring ways were undiscovered by Euro-Americans, who customarily believed there was no such thing as Native American civilization. In fact, Sweeney continues, "the perception of Native life was not cultured but stunted and static." And while this perception persisted tragically as colonization deepened its genocidal grips on Native people, movement away from such tragic perceptions of culture did not occur "until the birth of cultural anthropology in the late nineteenth and early twentieth centuries" (p. 8).

Such critical notions of culture, as Sweeney (2021) alluded, are noteworthy in the field of anthropology since it has experienced difficult treatment to this juncture of the book, and it has been the gift of cultural anthropology and research by the likes of Jesuit priest and more modern anthropologist Michael Steltenkamp (1982) that has created more dialogic space among faith perspectives such as the monotheistic notion of God he points as appearing

> to have existed … carefully identified with natural features so much a part of daily life. And even though this may sound as little more than a pantheon of spirit-entities comprising Native systems of religious thought, zealous Catholics might be reminded of their own regard for, or entreaty of, saints and angels. The truth is that something more profound seems to have been operative which neither caricature really admits. Both traditions reveal a persistent belief in the existence of a mediating, personal assistance which is supernatural, or wonderous. (p. 94)

Fair enough, in terms of comparisons and contrasts made across spiritual dimensions in which considerations were levied, pagan and otherwise, and also between Christian denominations. Yet, when it comes to the response from the Native community, Steltenkamp offered that traditionally, Native people

> have not constructed boundary-lines for behavior and thought the same as we have. Indian groups did not, as a whole, discriminate between spiritual and non-religious pursuits. Dividing the two would be a meaningless fabrication because the life-cycle was perceived as a sacred, ongoing, and inter-connected process. Theoretically, at least, Christians expose the same. (p. 86)

And finally, relative to this portion of the chapter, the impact of early anthropology and other perceptions of Native spiritual practice and culture overall by seminal historical phenomena, such as the Ghost Dance, stand as examples. Native people thought such a dance would restore Native culture from the death grip of colonial genocide. Warren (2015) rightly points to historical phenomena like the Ghost

Dance as an anecdotal practice to be resisted in terms of positioning it "within the non-progressive/progressive binary ...." Further, as Warren highlights when referencing the warning of "many scholars," singular phenomena like the Ghost Dance

> [are] a poor tool for understanding Indian motivations ... it divides Indians into two camps: one objectively refusing all change and purportedly destined to be swept aside, the other supposedly willing to assimilate to the American order and 'progress' toward whiteness ... Indians regularly confounded these expectations by combining old and new in novel formulations, mapping out alternate strategies to remain Indians while accomplishing other goals—and nowhere more so than in the Ghost Dance. (p. 145)

Similar to Black Elk and the complexity of him speaking to John Neihardt and others, including his great-great-great (great) grandson Maka, there still is a regular confounding of expectations by Native people in terms of tradition and new formulations, mapping out alternative strategies to remain Native. Additional examples and stories must be accessed of those non-Natives who remained in most persistent contact with Black Elk, Lakota people, and missionaries.

STORIES OF MISSIONARIES

With a sense of colonizing Christianity established, and the influence of social sciences like anthropology fueling fires of paganism and other "savage"-like descriptors of Native people, essentially crafting a narrative far exceeding the reality of Native culture, there were additional stories. Some of these stories stemmed from particular missionaries who were both precariously fueling such fires and periodically transcending the rapidly forming colonial Christian narrative by actually seeking to discern deeper Native spirituality and other customs through trusting and lasting relationships. While rafts of research exist to demonstrate the work of many other denominations' missionaries, for this book, a particular group of missionaries, the Jesuit priests primarily from Germany, will be highlighted as an example of those who both straddled the colonization of Christianity and attempted a decolonized approach.

The Jesuits, who served the Plain region of North America where Black Elk and the Lakota people resided, were known through Native translation as the Black Robes or more accurately Black Gowns. These were an exiled group from Germany, which was experiencing rebellion from the bottom up, like other European countries during the mid-1800s (Taylor, 2019/2021). In this upheaval, Jesuits left as refugees from their homeland to North America to only be in community with Native people who were also refugees from their own homelands, if not prisoners of war confined to camp-like reservations (Zielinski, 2020). Both groups, while distinctive in a number of ways, had a common bond of not knowing English well, which was the dominant colonial language in which all manner of education was to be obtained, including religious instruction. This common bond, with the acknowledgment of imperfection given some of the colonial measures levied by the Jesuits, was the basis for some common understanding, if not posited trust, as Maka shared through his own family stories.

These stories shared are not without blemish, as both Natives and Jesuits tried to navigate the chasm of language and custom. A particular story shared that nearly derailed the Jesuits' relationship, not only with Black Elk but also with the Lakota people, were encounters with some Jesuits who perceived Native religion more as Shamanistic Animism. Both John Neihardt's daughter Hilda (1995) and Maka (2021–2022) recount a specific encounter symbolic of such tension, when Black Elk attempted to heal a sick child as a "youthful medicine man." A Jesuit priest who also came to pray and heal "grabbed young Black Elk and pulled him rudely outside. Then he took Black Elk's sacred rattle, threw it to the ground, and stamped on it, admonishing the surprised young man that he should never use such 'heathen' objects again …" (H. Neihardt, 1995, pp. 88–89). Maka adds more vivid and emotional description handed down from family stories by recounting the encounter between Black Elk and the Jesuit priest, who admonished him:

> "Devil be gone." Or, "Satan be gone." And that's a moment that even his [Black Elk's] own daughter said that he never liked to talk about. Well, there's a reason why he didn't like to talk about that, probably because it was painful, and certain parts gave him pause. So he was living in a reality, where he was trying to understand what it meant to be a Lakota person in this new existence that was very different …. (Personal communication/ interview, 2021–2022)

With language being a somewhat common, and often perplexing matter, in terms of Jesuits and Lakota people learning English practically simultaneously, additional stories through Maka's family demonstrated an additional gesture by Jesuits. This particular gesture transcended the relationship of exiles learning English to a quality of "more trust" afforded to the "Black Robes" as the result of an effort by the Jesuits to learn and be able to communicate in the Lakota language. This conveyed to the Lakota people in general and healers such as Black Elk, in particular, a desire on the part of the Jesuits to build relationships "more inclined to starting off as equals … all in the span of these years, which showed extreme commitment to learning the language and communicating with … elderly medicine men." One of the distinctive elements concerning the Jesuits, according to Maka's familial accounts through story and subsequent study as a scholar in his own right (thus illuminating this "affinity"), was an academic inclination of Jesuits to have "dialogue about faith, and intercultural senses of faith, and belief in God." So exceptional was (and in some senses still is today) this affinity in Maka's recount of story and study, in that he said, "I think if the Black Robes weren't around … he [Black Elk] may not have had the same kind of engagement and even theological depth, that he was able to get…" (Personal communication/interview, 2021–2022)

Even with this constructive development, despite a colonized Christianity, were glimmers of coexistence showing promise. Although it was not without overwhelming eruptions of historical trauma embodied in seminal years of tragedy symbolized in just over two weeks, "In the moon of the Popping Trees [December]," when the Lakota people heard that Sitting Bull was dead. News carried fast from the reaches of Sitting Bull's death at this camp on the Grand River to the Agency [Pine Ridge], where another story of historical trauma was brewing, as Neihardt (1970) gleaned from Black Elk: "soldiers were camped there too, but they did not bother us because we did not dance." Black Elk recounted further that as the news permeated the people at Pine Ridge, the people "were starving and many of them were sick.…" And while this news settled upon a starving people, soldiers began to surround people who were assembled "by Porcupine Butte and took them to Wounded Knee Creek." As Black Elk witnessed somewhat later and many experienced sooner is what most would today call the Massacre at Wounded Knee, the "next morning … all at once we heard shooting over there across the hills … They kept on shooting fast … They are butchering over there …" (p. 246).

As desperate and traumatic as the histories of both Sitting Bull's death and Wounded Knee prevailed on a people, whose stories started this book as exceptional and now near extinction due to many examples of massacre such as Wounded Knee, enter again the Black Robes. The Black Robes offered refuge to fallen Lakota people who sought refuge in many natural settings in the frozen land of Pine Ridge in late 1890, but also the Holy Rosary Mission, where bullet holes remain from soldiers who chased Native people seeking refuge at the Mission. One can only imagine the gathering of a traumatized people at a mission like Holy Rosary, with the Black Robe Jesuits, who "more than any other group, filled the spiritual gulf created by Wounded Knee, and they did so by occupying a middle ground between the old word and the new." Both Natives and Jesuits shared the story of "exile from one's native land.... [and] Pain and suffering—their acceptance and endurance—were the nexus of both Catholic and Lakota identity" (Jackson, 2016, pp. 351–353).

This sense of the intricacy of relationship in the midst of a colonized Christianity is best summarized in this section regarding stories of missionaries by Surgirtharajah, who described how missionaries often occupied an "ambivalent social location in a colonial situation." Further, the author articulated how missionaries "participated in colonial practice and often shared the Western view of the essentialized native." And with the imbued nature of this practice, there was still a practice that transcended such colonialism with a particular type of

> missionary work that put them into close communal contact with the colonized ... often influenced or required ... to engage in native cultural practices and language, which allowed them to see the colonized as human beings. Despite their inability to extract themselves completely from colonial practices, this contact also led missionaries to critique colonialism explicitly ... [creating a] "dissidence," where the Christian narrative is used by missionaries to challenge colonialism from within the system. (as cited in Costello, 2005, p. 17)

Black Elk was at the epicenter of this sagacity of close communal contact, bringing his own version of "salvation history ... at least partially influenced by retreats he attended with the Jesuits... from the Ignatian Spiritual Exercises. The retreats were called *hamble iciyope* 'crying for a vision'... Black Elk attended eight retreats ..." (Costello, 2005, p. 132). Overall, Black Elk and other Lakota people may have felt this opportunity for such contact, due to the Jesuits' ability to stress the "universality of the [Catholic] Church," whether the relationship between Native Americans and Mary via an "ethnic connection to the Mexican Native Americans...." Or, this sense that both "Catholics and Lakotas believed that people had visions and also that supernatural beings appeared to people ... The Jesuits tended to accept as inspired those dreams and visions that led people to the Church" (Enochs, 1996, p. 122).

Again, with full consideration of the ills brought also by missionary endeavors, possibly undervalued is the discernment of the Jesuits' understanding of the problems of the Lakota and the desire to advocate for justice and change in areas like "government policy ... in a sea of white apathy and hostility" (Costello, 2005, pp. 25–26, 33–34). An important point summarizing this chapter, and one of the more telling qualities of this particular approach to missionary work that broke some bonds of a colonialist Christianity, was "by retaining the indigenous language for mission activity, the Jesuits asserted (perhaps unknowingly) a claim in opposition to colonial ideology...." Noteworthy priests symbolic of such opposition to colonial ideology, and still mentioned in various Native communities, with possible consideration of ways in which missionary activity may be considered, are "Francis Craft, who was of Mohawk decent, [who] may have participated in the Sun Dance.... Craft later compared the Sun Dance to the Eucharist ... [and] called the government-banned Ghost Dance 'quite Catholic and even edifying,'" and Pierre Jean De Smet, who is often noted for saying that "Native American religion and politics were well-developed cultural institutions ... their intelligence was 'far above the medium of uneducated white men'" (Costello, 2005, pp. 25–26, 33–34, 38).

With the wisdom uttered by two Catholic missionary priests who, no doubt are not without blemish, but do stand as having taken exceptional and distinctive approaches to their ministry. Some of which may be relevant today in terms of ways in which consideration of cultural and spiritual convergence are possible and could play a role in cultural healing overall. What is key with models of convergence and healing past and present, that surface or are provoked in a positive sense through good intercultural dialogue and scholarship, is that the Native American "intelligence" De Smet made note of is central and prioritized "far above the medium of uneducated white men."

This sense of centrality and priority is the logic behind Black Elk's life speaking "that much ... more," meaning more than those who have spoken most over the centuries, primarily "white men." It is important to recall earlier the centrality and priority of Native voices here, not at the exclusion of non-Native voices. Rather, flipped from past precedence where mainly non-Native voices were central to the story of Native people, and now Native people's stories are told primary to their account, and others, who could also be primary, may also be a secondary source speaking to the overall accurate and authentic value of Native stories. It is the hope, if this logic is only clear to this point by the author of this book, that the following chapter as an example of Native voice and story more central to the way in which Black Elk's life speaks in his own words and through decedents and Native people at large will better clarify, in an attempt to elucidate steps to cultural healing.

CHAPTER 3

Stories from Black Elk's Family Tree Speaking "That Much ... More"

Julie Wishmeyer/Shutterstock.com

Twiss (2015) aptly noted that when it comes to the value of stories, fundamentally, "stories are people, people are stories, and stories are alive." Ironically, and often unfortunately, such stories are "never fully explained." Paradoxically, while the non-Native community may undervalue or be skeptics of the reliability and validity of such stories, the contrary would seem to be evident, when considering issues germane to this book, for example, in terms of Black Elk's life speaking, Twiss also noted an essential clarification regarding the power and influence of the story, not necessarily lying in the "exact correctness of its telling, but in the life of the 'teller' and in the 'telling' (difficult to nuance with a link on a page; Twiss, 2015, p. 191).

So, it is these stories, and the context established leading to this point undergirding such stories, that have established a foundation for what Maka, via a series of interviews, has gleaned for most of his life just surpassing three decades. And while some of those stories have been already shared, critical to the discernment of Black Elk's life speaking possibly fully and more accessible to a more comprehensive range of people, a helpful metaphor is that of the family tree and its various branches that most families tend to identify generally and more particularly situationally.

Maka is situated in the branch of the Black Elk family tree that follows from Ben Black Elk, the son of Black Elk. And while this branch has thoughts about Black Elk himself, ranging from traditional Lakota healer to devout Catholic convert, it is the alchemy of these stories relative to Black Elk's genesis as a seminal healer among his people that Maka seems to embody when he shares,

> that's where certainly my own feelings come into it, being a Lakota person myself, who is Catholic, being a descendant of his, coming from the branch of his family who believes that his Catholicism was inauthentic. If you're familiar with that whole split, in terms of his descendants and how they feel about his Catholicism. And so, that has informed certainly my own sense of who he was and what my family told about him. (Personal communication/interview, 2021–2022)

This lineage was also carried by Maka's maternal grandmother Charlotte and mother by eventual adoption, or as Maka put it "technically its three greats [grandparent]… legally it's two greats … because I was adopted by my grandparents." As such, Charlotte is the daughter of Henry Black Elk and Agnes Hollow Horn. "Henry Black Elk is the son of Benjamin Black Elk who is the son of (Nicholas) Black Elk" (Personal communication/interview, 2021–2022). As was depicted earlier in this book, Charlotte no doubt echoed this family branch of thought in terms of the more traditional Lakota view of Black Elk and was consistent with Ben Black Elk in terms of skepticism regarding Black Elk's full embrace of the Catholic religion. This sense was highlighted with a helpful overview by Maka who assisted with making me as the interviewer familiar with Black Elk, his descendants' thoughts about him, and the condition in which he ascended by elaborating that,

> there's one branch of the family that believes that his Catholicism was really just more a product of the time. I just imagine that when he was a young man first entering reservation life, reservation life was incredibly restrictive, moving was restricted, the ability to access resources was really restricted. Poverty was just incredibly high, and freedom was incredibly low.

Whereas there wasn't a complete consensus among the lineal descendants of Black Elk, according to Maka, there appeared to be consensus surrounding perception of him as "someone who was deeply invested in understanding God, trying to help other people understand … and a deep interest in how people thought about God."

Even as Black Elk's spiritual prowess crossed all familial branches in terms of consensus, it is important to highlight another agreement among family which was "his academic interest" (Personal communication/interview, 2021–2022).

Academic interest remained true throughout this branch of the Black Elk family tree, as was highlighted earlier in Maka's undergraduate and graduate education, his (grand) mother Charlotte's profound cultural education and advocacy for Lakota people, and his (grand) father's background in theology with partial Catholic seminary training, then an engineering background "designing missile components for an aerospace company in Los Angeles" (Greider, 1987, pp. 12–13).

Together, with now a grandson turned son through legal adoption in the later 1980s, Gerald's spiritual development in the Catholic Church, and Charlotte's as a traditional Lakota were impactful within their immediate family circle, and more broadly on Pine Ridge in terms of advocacy. Gerald recounted upon his return from Los Angeles disillusioned with his engineering work, after several years of discernment during the "upheaval of the Sixties," was resolved to reject "the assimilation thing," and said to one another feeling similarly, "It's good to be an Indian. We're going to be Lakota, whatever that is." Gerald, along with the influence of Charlotte and others, found this deeper quest for cultural identity, complimentary to his own Catholic formation and the "tremendously rich spiritual heritage that I was part of by inheritance. I'd been kept from it. Now I had to learn it" (Greider, 1987, pp. 12–13). Learn in earnest they did, as both those associated by marriage or directly from the Ben Black Elk branch of the Black Elk family tree, continue(d) to do in the person of Maka. This imparting of cultural learning is evident in Maka, who is now also a cultural advocate, and in turn shares such learning, with the Pine Ridge Reservation in association with Holy Rosary Mission and Red Cloud School, thereby carefully navigating intense, contemporary cultural tensions such as the impact of residential boarding schools and unmarked gravesites.

Regarding this academic interest more generally, both Maka and Steltenkamp (1993) sound similar thoughts of Black Elk developing a "worldview that included more than the Lakota Reservation experience. This background provided him with new perspectives … that later proved advantageous in his work as a catechist. His travels gave experiential substance to what he said" (p. 69). According to Sweeney (2021), experiences of travel may be one of the motives for expanding his horizons and moving beyond the restrictive nature of the ever-constricting reservation life—though many in his community perceived his ventures with skepticism, envy, if not outright disdain according to Sweeney. Black Elk seems to have believed that sojourns with Buffalo Bill's Wild West Show, for example, were a good idea, "'because I might learn some secret … that would help my people somehow … Maybe if I could see the great world of the Wasichu [Non Native people—mainly white], I could understand how to bring the sacred hoop together and make the tree bloom again at the center of it'" (p. 36).

So, motive creates opportunity, which echoes why some of the Black Elk descendants view Black Elk as an opportunist in terms of his conversion to Christianity, namely Catholicism. In fact, according to Powers and Rice, they see Black Elk's motives relative to Christianity "…as a strategy to protect his people … dealing with a conscious strategy rather than an inevitable process (syncretism)…" in the attempt to "preserv[e] traditional values and institutions" (as cited in Holler, 1995, p. 207). Steltenkamp (2009) also echoes familial stories, noting that when it came to Black Elk's exceptional ability as a healer to be a medium for visions, they were "…neither parochially Lakota nor insularly Catholic … they entailed a cross-fertilization of Christian and Lakota traditions that was enriching to both …" (p. 123).

This ability to be a "medium of visions" persists from Black Elk's youth through adulthood, both among his people and while traveling abroad. Steltenkamp (2009) notes further that it is "not surprising" that Christian themes and images should appear in this vision, considering his familiarity with Christian teaching gained while in Europe. And by bridging his experience abroad with that of a newer spiritual phenomenon associated with the Ghost Dance, which promised a return to exceptionality and a release from the shackles of colonization, "…Black Elk's vision was the crucified wanikiye (the man standing against a tree with arms outstretched and wounds in his hands)" (pp. 63–64).

BLACK ELK FAMILY TREE STORIES: "TRUE CONVERT"

If the complexities of stories prior to colonial contact, during contact, and now within the wake of such contact, particularly mired in the impact of trauma were enough to put a bow on the discernment of Black Elk, Lakota culture, and implications of survivance today, then this book could conclude.

Nevertheless, as with other misconceptions drawn about cultural engagement, complexities, though identified, seem to be avoided or denied for a variety of reasons. Reasons usually relating to Native culture's ability not only to lend discernment to historical context but also to present and future implications. The same holds for this alternate branch of the Black Elk family tree due to the colonization of Christianity and self-attested, providential reasons. Black Elk's daughter Lucy represents an adaptative development in Native spirituality which

Maka identified as the "complete opposite" of others related to Black Elk because she felt that,

> his Catholicism was a true conversion. And that ultimately, prior to his death, he then spoke against the Lakota tradition and felt that he really fully embraced his Catholic faith in that, these traditions that he grew up with weren't worth keeping, he renounces that. (Personal communication/interview, 2021–2022)

And while Maka shared Lucy's zeal for the Catholic faith and inspiration regarding Black Elk's conversation, his take on Black Elk's conversion is somewhat more tempered than Lucy's. In fact, he likely represents the most nuanced sense of Black Elk's life speaking today to Native and non-Native people alike. Maka shared that he did not think Black Elk ever "renounced his traditions," rendering his conversion to Catholicism somehow "inauthentic." Rather, Maka pointed to Black Elk as a

> complex person, who was really existing in a place ahead of his time, where he had figured out how to be a Lakota person who was also Catholic, and that he didn't find conflict in those things. He saw conflict all around him, but I don't think he felt a personal conflict within himself. (Personal communication/ interview, 2021–2022)

David Treuer (2019) contextualized even more succinctly the complexity of Black Elk as a person when recounting Black Elk's life when "the fighting was over," Treuer said, "his life was not."

> Black Elk married and had a family. He converted to Catholicism and become a catechist at the Catholic Church in Pine Ridge. Many indigenous prefer not to think about Black Elk's later years and consider his conversion as some kind of surrender, a confirmation of the old ways were in fact dead. Maybe, maybe not. Black Elk was determined to live and adapt. That doesn't make him less of an Indian, as I see it; it makes him more of one. (p. 450)

Jackson (2016) delved deeper into an analysis of family thoughts regarding who articulated this complexity when drawing attention to Lucy Black Elk's concern with "Ben [Black Elk] at the helm." Jackson went on to stipulate, "Given the later direction of his thought, he may have shown too much interest in the old ways to make Lucy comfortable…." In fact, Jackson elaborated further that Lucy had "come of age" at a time when her father's old religion was banned and Lakota language and culture had been vigorously suppressed in Catholic and government schools. Overall, similar to what may be evident in any son or daughter honored with the legacy of a father, Lucy Black Elk was in fact "proud of her catechist father: he was an honored man, and through him, she had community standing" (p. 413).

Steltenkamp (1993), who had significant contact with Lucy Black Elk prior to her passing, thought that following Black Elk's death in 1950, the funeral closed the book on Black Elk's life "and further illumination seemed left pretty much to anyone's speculation…." Yet, Steltenkamp happened to meet Lucy Black Elk at Holy Rosary Mission while he was teaching at the school during what he identifies as a smoke beak. It was a needed break, most likely, as Steltenkamp had been desperately doing his best to enliven a sense of Native culture while attempting to relate Black Elk's story to students at Red Cloud Indian High School. On a bench outside the mission school, a woman shared, "When I was a little girl, I came to school here, and so did my brother Ben…." It was at that moment that Steltenkamp surmised that the "illumination of Black Elk's life was in fact alive and not left to speculation due to the chance encounter with Black Elk's only surviving child…." Consequently, researchers from that point on, including myself and interviews with Maka, share his sentiment that such encounters with Black Elk's lineal descendants provide a critical and distinctive, if not imperative, opportunity "to help … understand more deeply just who her father was" (1993, p. xviii).

It may be possible in summarizing this portion of the chapter, that Steltenkamp represents a second generation of those privileged to lean into the sacred stories of culture bearers such as Lucy Black Elk, similar to arguably the first generation like John Neihardt and Joseph Epes Brown, who heard stories directly from Black Elk. There is a temptation to posit that the stories shared by Maka indicate another emerging generation of culture bearers and/or scholars in the vintage of Black Elk speaking. As tempting as this may be, it may be premature, even with what Gustafson (1997) observed how common it is today for

> enlightened people to talk about the Indigenous peoples throughout the world as keeps of the land … What we must now realize … is we also of the technological world are indigenous peoples at some forgotten place within ourselves and, at one time, had a living indigenous past with a sense of intimately belonging to the earth. Indigenous really refers to an attitude and a way of life that respects the unity and relationship of all things on earth. (pp. 78–79)

Gustafson (1997) concluded forgetting such roots can result in "sentimentalizing" millions of Indigenous people of the world, thereby creating another culturally binary fissure "that keeps projections of our own forgotten ancestral life actively placed on 'them.' At the same time, it is true we have much to learn from such known keepers of the land about what we have forgotten" (pp. 78–79).

If Jungian overtones have not become explicit via Gustafson (1997) at this point, then more overtly Gustafson divines Jung and his seminal work *Man and His Symbols* as Jung echoed the plight of an enlightened people as a "modern condition" in which a "scientific understanding has grown, so our world has become dehumanized. Man feels ... isolated ... because he is no longer involved in nature and has lost his emotional 'unconscious identity' with natural phenomena" (p. 102). Jung (1961) carried this sense of a lost "unconscious identity" further, and contemplation of dignity, in his visit to North America while immersed with Native people like the "Pueblo Indians." Jung realized a non-Native response to a Native way of life comes out of "sheer envy," and "self-justification," where the

> meaning of our own lives as it is formulated by our reason, we cannot help but see our poverty ... we are obliged to smile at the Indians' naivete and to plume ourselves on our cleverness; for otherwise we would discover how impoverished and down at the heels we are. Knowledge does not enrich us; it removes us more and more from the mythic world in which we were once at home by right of birth. (p. 252)

Jung would suggest a sense of a "symbolic phenomena" has slowly been lost in terms of enrichment. Nevertheless, Jung has also implied such phenomena is not entirely lost because in order for knowledge to "enrich us," there would need to be a synthesis of what is perceived as knowledge and the "the mystical word." This holistic perspective could be a sagacity of knowledge, not only of a "home by right of birth" per see but also all those who can have a shared sense of this home, most importantly via the transcendent perspective.

Intermixed in this complex intercultural milieu in terms of ancestry imagined, forgotten, and posited upon others, is an emerging generation David Treuer (2019) called "digital Indians" who are more and more quickly "closing the gaps that separate us. In past eras, it might have been enough for Indians merely to survive ... we are using modernity in the best possible way: to work together and to heal what was broken" (pp. 442–443). Treuer commented that this generation, though wise beyond their years due to direct engagements, represents the "biggest shift" as a "kind of collective determination to do more" than simply survive.

Rather, Treuer viewed this as an active, engaged presence and at times resistance, also known as survivance has a plethora of contemporary examples in education, art, and activism such as the Dakota Access Pipeline and Enbridge Pipeline protests. Historically, this is not the first time such expressions and assertions of survivance have been expressed, nevertheless, it would seem the impact of more contemporary "collective determination" has manifested itself beyond Native culture in the broader mosaic of culture at large. One other force may be at work as this current narrative generation has been identified prophetically as the generation with an impact as Treuer alluded to.

Furthermore, in almost apocalyptic language associated with the environment and relations among cultures, it would appear the staying power of this current generation of "digital Indians" would seem as equally imperative to the present and future human condition at large as a reminiscent historical and tragic risk of an often involuntary, colonized infused slip from survivance to survival. It may be bold to suggest that Native culture is central to culture at large with its historical scars and present challenges; nevertheless, again this is the point posited with the book in terms of Black Elk's life speaking directly and through many various sources such as Native first and foremost, and most importantly his decedents, in terms of stories speaking "that much ... more ...," offering centrality to the discernment of our collective historical stories in terms of cultural healing.

BLACK ELK FAMILY TREE STORIES: "THE TRUTH SOMEWHERE IN THE MIDDLE"

Another key focus lending stories to the possibility of the possible central role of cultural healing in terms of the way Black Elk's life speaks "that much ... more," are inherent, additional, complex, accounts of family history. By recalling sections through this book where both Maka's (grand) mother and (grand) father were formed distinctively within their own journeys as Lakota people, it seems such recollection suggests a convergence of these distinctive formative qualities in the person of Maka. Even with the prior accounts of stories building this sense via the words shared by both Maka and his immediate family, this formation continues as Black Elk's life continues to speak "that much ... more," in an emerging generation of his legacy.

With this perspective, context is always critical in terms of looking back to consider the present and future implications of such a legacy in terms of the meaning of "that much ... more," relative to Black Elk's life speaking through a familial legacy and dare suggest by way of adoption. For example, when familial stories were told, by those descendants of Black Elk, relative to the perception of John Neihardt's book *Black Elk Speaks*, some would comment generally that there was a limited, in terms of that "level of spirituality discussed is this much." Specifically, Maka shared, the accounting of such stories would entail gestures of hands or fingers showing a small gap of just how much Neihardt's book captured, while "living our lives as Lakota people, are aware of and experience this much … more." This assertion would be accompanied by a gesture that "grew bigger than what even Neihardt was able to capture" (Personal communication/interview, 2021–2022). This same account was captured in an interview when another researcher asked Charlotte Black Elk about her great-grandfather and the book *Black Elk Speaks*:

> To tell you the truth, I've never had the inclination to sit down and read it … Being related to someone like Black Elk brings a sense of responsibility that's not very gratifying sometimes, especially when you're a kid. I guess I never really felt I had to read it. As my Grandpa Ben told me, the book is about this much (thumb and forefinger an inch apart) and you already know this much (arms wide apart). (as cited in Frazier, 2000, p. 119)

As often is the enticement, with various researchers and Neihardt's seminal work (1932/1971), is to critique such works with the luxury of hindsight. Maka places this consideration of Neihardt's work, in the cannon of Black Elk research, as being the first generation of those who encountered individuals like Black Elk, and the way in which his life spoke, and is speaking, given the responsibly of great stewardship and consideration with such words. Maka shared that culturally there is "a revitalization movement toward traditional, spiritual life," which is to be credited and honored along with the way in which, "Black Elk himself continued to teach those traditions while he was alive, and the book *Black Elk Speaks* really documented our traditional practices and beliefs, and were major ways in which people were able to go back to those traditions and revitalize those efforts" (Personal communication/interview, 2021–2022).

The John Neihardt research debate, within the canon of Black Elk research, continues, in terms of where his seminal work *Black Elk Speaks* situated within the discernment of Black Elk per se, but also Native spirituality in general. Regardless of positions in the date and/or cannon of Black Elk research and understanding, there are some foundational points offered to build upon not only regulated solely to Black Elk and Native spirituality but possibly also to the advancement and support of Native survivance and overall, as this book also hopes to perpetuate, cultural healing. First, due to *Black Elk Speaks*, as a descendant of Black Elk himself, Maka stipulated that due to this documentation and account of such Native practices and beliefs, there is a reference point from which efforts in terms of revitalization piercing centuries of colonization can occur. Therefore, this revitalization shows promise as inertia for Native people to reestablish more of an authentic cultural identity. Second, how Black Elk speaks and to what end does not all rest on the shoulders of Neihardt's work, but in company with his work, via additional accounts. The additional accounts would include Native scholarship that often, ironically, is left out of such accounting of Native culture, particularly when considering the impact of the "that much … more," Black Elk speaks. With the critical consistent, additional Native voice and scholarship, then more effectively such collective scholarship, can enter a contemporary dialogue with the next generation of Native people like Maka, who can by example and scholarship, discover ways in which accounts of Native culture broadly, and in particular spiritually, have present-day relevance as a means to survivance in the face of oppression and colonization.

Maka presented his great-great-(great) grandfather Black Elk as someone historically, culturally, and presently imminent, whose life spoke and speaks today as a "straight up theologian … medium, paragon, medicine man …" to Native people. In addition, he shared the spirit of the Lakota saying Mitákuye Oyás'iŋ all are related. And similar to the spiritual path that all embark upon, Black Elk included, there is a development toward what Maka identified as a "truth somewhere in the middle," which is a life modeled and exemplified by Black Elk and Maka for that matter in this author's earlier account from his family experiences. Maka went on further to share Black Elk's spiritual journey in this fashion, as he discerned through his own familial ties:

> So Black Elk, I think early on, along with a lot of his fellow medicine men contemporaries, would have been people who were engaged in theological discussion about God, with priests, with each other. And Black Elk was just a paragon among them, he did have a way of expressing his visions, which we believe. We know in Lakota tradition; visions are directly coming from our creator. That they're for medicine men to interpret, but that they are coming from God. Yeah. Just the way you would think of an educated Catholic, the worldview of the prophets. And so that's what they're given that status of. But Black Elk was a luminary in that regard. His ability to express deep theological concepts, in these really beautiful and powerful ways, was unparalleled in his time. I think that's just what makes him unique. I think even for my own family … disagreed that he was authentically Catholic (Personal communication/interview, 2021–2022).

Once again, the tension is evident in terms of a community in response to the pressures of outside forces relative to colonization, and then internally as to what the response may be, as developed throughout this book, in terms of viewing Black Elk. Views and tensions recounted of Black Elk such as an "instigator of traditional revitalization in traditional ceremony and practices and belief" or "venerated ... being someone who took from that prayer life and was this bridge between cultures and fake traditions" or even more intensely as a "traitor ... giving up these details of our traditions, opened us up to white scrutiny," which Maka shared came from a "space where our traditions and our ceremonies were outlawed and banned and even persecuted with punishment." These various views and tensions reveal a very real question to ponder while potentially allied, Native and non-Native, in a struggle with varying tension, equipped with the familial stories of Black Elk speaking to an ascendancy through challenges of survivance: "Why would we ever want to reveal those [traditions, ceremonies] again to the people who condemn [outlawed and banned and even persecuted with punishment] them?" (Personal communication/interview, 2021–2022).

Despite the risk of sharing such intimate cultural revelations, Maka shared further, this sacred way of spirituality, toward this "truth somewhere in the middle" is, as he described for some, a "secret. And so, he's [Black Elk] seen as someone who betrayed that" (Personal communication/interview, 2021–2022). At first blush, confusion can rein in terms of how such a significant person to a culture can be perceived as something so alienating as a traitor, yet perspective is key when reflecting on other cultural and spiritual accounts of people who come along within other cultural groups and attempt to be such a "straight up theologian ... paragon" or even paradoxically a "lodestar," for example. Whereas there are many more examples to offer with this book's limited space, it should be widely held as an example in the story of Jesus of Nazareth comes to mind as another example of someone who was also afforded descriptors, and yet confusion, tension, and yes metanoia still pervade today, as all stories are held in and to account. Maybe that's the point, the stories continue with enough room for tension to exist for even nuanced stories to evolve with the trust of a kind of generational stewardship.

CHAPTER 4

Stories of Canonization and Native Saints

Nancy Bauer/Shutterstock.com

The call for generational stewardship expressed in Chapter 3 remains. The call is mainly due to the fact that, even though Black Elk died in 1950, and other significant spiritual leaders well before, their legacies still play out within a shroud of tension that runs the gambit of transformation to violence. What is more, with the potential canonization of Black Elk as a saint by the Catholic Church, currently identified in the early process as a Servant of God, such ranges of tension are currently unfolding. The question is, will history be a guide in the face of such tension and be a product of cultural healing, or will the more tired and historically traumatic story persevere? Maka shared the reality of both:

> ...there are people, who again, see him as Catholic and then when he becomes a saint, that would be a validation of that. If and when he becomes a saint. And then there are people who see him as a product of service, a very complex history. That he, in some ways, is a sellout traitor. Sold our traditions to this highest bidder who then made profit off of it via the book. Makes profit off of our traditions and our stories and our beliefs, and to see him as having basically failed us in a way by doing so. So there's really a gamete of views and I think if Black Elk were to become

a canonized saint, that would only intensify. For sure. And there are people who believe the Catholic Church is doing this on purpose because this is another way for them to continue the evangelization process, and to try and sneak Catholicism back in again, to people who don't want to.... (Personal communication/interview, 2021–2022)

Hitherto, with the dire possibility of tension unfolding that could replicate the trauma of history, Maka shared there may be hope in this process of canonization of Black Elk, as possibly all of the thoughts of Black Elk, embodied in this current tension of canonization, could be held differently in terms of a constructive process embracing all tension. Whereas, "Catholics who have no idea about Lakota people, [Lakota] history, are having now to confront it in a way that they haven't been asked to, up until that point." Maka referenced the example of Native American Saint Kateri Tekakwitha as a process approximately ten years ago that held promise for a productive balance of tensions. Yet, as he mentioned, his "feeling is that her canonization, even though I find her story personally compelling and beautiful," he also shared that the "social impact" may have not had the reach as intended with possible cultural missteps regarding historical accuracies of her life to even accounts during the actual canonization where most likely unintended cultural faux pas occurred:

[T]here are pictures of that celebration, there were these Catholic nuns in full habit with them were wearing these sort of costume store-bought headdresses with orange and green and blue feathers and yellow feathers. I was like, "No! Why did you do that?" And I think that spoke to a lot of what other Catholic people have said, "Yes. We want to celebrate to Saint Kateri." But in a way that made her ... That cheapened, to an extent, her potential. [It] communicated to us that, still the wrong lessons are being given to non ... Catholic people, that this felt more like a costume to them.... (Personal communication/interview, 2021–2022)

This account, coupled with some scholarly regarding motives behind the canonization of Native saints, is why some, even Kateri Tekakwitha's own Mohawk people regard her, and one could speculate the cause of Native saints in general, as a process that is "romanticized ..., fictionalized like Disneyland ..." And while skepticism abounds, Bonaparte countered with a list of Mohawk advocates who "have been here strongest advocates ..." (as cited in Thiel & Vecsey, 2013, p. 22). And similar to Black Elk in terms of the way in which stories have furthered the way in which he speaks that much more, so for Kateri Tekakwitha, as "stories about Kateri have circulated for generations among members of some family" (Thiel & Vecsey, 2012, p. 107).

Jacob (2016) also explored "contestations and contradictions that surround Saint Kateri" (p. 9). Although many have exhausted the story of this Indigenous saint canonized by the Catholic Church, Jacob seems to have carved out something more exceptional as an Indigenous scholar may be best poised in terms of explicating Kateri as "a powerful woman figure ...," without being mindful of the portrayal by "historical Jesuit accounts leaving her 'heathen' people to live among French Jesuits, so that she could dedicate her life to Jesus Christ." Further, Jacob chronicled the Catholic Church is "narrative" regarding Kateri as one that "situated Indigenous peoples at the bottom of a racial hierarchy, and in doing so further justified the 'Manifest Destiny' that fueled colonial policies ..." (pp. 10–11).

The varying "contestations and contradictions" surrounding Kateri Tekakwitha, and in a parallel fashion Black Elk, is part of what has, and most likely continues to "disrupt essentializing dichotomies," due to an interest that "means so many different things to different peoples," and over the past three hundred years, "has become the most visible representation of Native American Catholicism." A representation, that Indigenous studies scholars have argued, and I would include Jacob as prominent here, who elaborated that it "is very important to Indigenous peoples...[as a] powerful figure who ... transforms Catholicism and provides ... allies with meaningful ways to center Indigenous culture within their spiritual practices ... as either 'Catholic' or 'Indigenous,'" but rather both/and "in a way that transforms their spiritual lives to have great meaning." Jacob (2016) called this process of inhibiting such a transformation as "indigenizing the Catholic Church," as a form of decolonization, defined by Wilson and Yellow Bird as

> the intelligent, calculated, and active resistance to the forces of colonialism that perpetuate the subjugation and/or exploitation of our minds, bodies, and lands, and ... is engaged for the ultimate purpose of overturning the colonial structure and realizing indigenous liberation. (pp. 10–11)

One example of the latter is the story of suffering that Kateri Tekakwitha embodies as a "role model and kin figure" (Jacob, 2016, p. 35), in terms of her struggles with debilitating illness at a young age, among other challenges facing her during a colonial period in which Indigenous women were maltreated. And within this embodiment of role model and the kin figure comes a broader understanding in need of elaboration—otherwise, an important social distinction may be lost on an ever-increasing demand on what something like kinship, which contains many role model means culturally. Gustafson (1997) pointed to the idea and practice of the nuclear family as a "cultural invention that puts an unfair emotional weight on all family members and is anything but native to the human psyche." Furthermore, he alluded to a revival of the nuclear family as a portion of the total puzzle when considering more holistically what kinship really means. Gustafson advocated for the extended family as what needs to be reclaimed, and Indigenous peoples are exemplars in terms of modeling this in terms of knowing "the place of inclusive family systems." He pointed to an example of how "even individuals not connected by blood ties will sometime be addressed by familial ties like 'uncle, aunt'…Under this model, a family included many people with intricate social and religious obligations and taboos. Many people in an extended family carried responsibility for raising a child" (pp. 112–113).

Whether the story of Kateri or other Indigenous, according to Million, these are communal stories that "arose from the relations in a way of life, not separately." In fact, Million extended this further into an even more contemporary context relative to Indigenous communities, with such role models and kin figures, can "shift the discourse from "how to heal from dysfunction" to "how to govern ourselves so that nations are empower as healthy people" (as cited in Jacob, 2016, p. 55). And in this shifting, catalyzed by the modeling of such figures such as Kateri, comes representative testimony expressed by many Native people whether during childhood or as an adult, when Kateri was introduced to them formally or informally, regardless of the pedagogical or formal catechesis, there was a mystical connection. Marvin Clifford from the Rosebud Reservation put it this way in an interview with researchers,

> Those other saints always seems to be far-off people from a far-off land but I could identify with Kateri Tekakwitha. She was an Indian. I didn't know about the Iroquois or the Mohawk because I never met an Indian from another tribe and we weren't taught about other cultures and stuff about other tribes. So all I knew was that she was Indian and it was good enough for me because I was assured there was a place in God's heart for Native people. (Thiel & Vecsey, 2012, pp. 171–172)

Anna Marie Sandoval (also interviewed) from the Navajo Reservation posed another connection inspired by her connection to Kateri,

> I really talk to her as an Indian, not as Saint Francis or another tribe or … some Anglo … This was an Indian … You know who we are. You know how we are. You know our clan system. This is

how I talk to her ... I really feel ... she understands ... she's
the one that really grasped ... Christianity like this, and when
you grasp something like that, you know that these people are
going to criticize you. But even in spirt of that, she kept that. She
wanted to believe in God ... But now when I pray to her I know
that I'm talking to a strong person ... it gives me strength ...
I have somebody that I can look up to in heaven.... (Thiel &
Vecsey, 2012, pp. 205–206)

Accordingly, the consideration of another Indigenous person like Black Elk
for canonization, with the lessons and example of the process leading to Kateri
Tekakwitha's ascendancy to sainthood, cultural context, fully brought to the light
of critique, is critical. An example of such a crucial, contextual critique is from a
prominent, scholarly voice on Black Elk, as a professed, Indigenous, religious in the
Catholic Church, Sister Theresa Archambault observed the critical connections of
struggles past and present, most notably when considering the impact of economic
frameworks like "Western capitalism." Archambault noted that,

Black Elk faced many hard choices: how to express himself in
a changed society; how to unify in himself diverse religious
traditions; how to survive economically in a world that no longer
valued his cultural gifts. We ... face similar decisions about how
to achieve our spiritual goals .... (as cited in Jacob, 2016, p. 57)

Another example of such a critique is via a "Mohawk repatriation of Kateri
Tekakwitha," by Mohawk author Darren Bonaparte, who argued that some of the
"traits Catholic missionaries praised in Kateri where indeed lessons she learned
of traditional matriarchal Mohawk longhouse culture" (as cited in Jacob, 2016,
p. 122). And while scholars such as Bonaparte and other aforementioned bring
to light such a critique, as Jacob (2016) keenly summarized, "historical–cultural
accuracy and understanding is not the central concern in the Catholic literature
about Kateri Tekakwitha" (p. 122). Such a seminal point when considering the
future disposition relative to the canonization of any Indigenous person let alone
Black Elk in terms of a shift in the literature, particularly Catholic and historical-
cultural accuracy. It would seem a primary catalyst for such a shift would be more
indigenous voices, scholarly and otherwise, which are slowly emerging, namely
Maka who mentioned in interviews his committee work with the U.S. Catholic
Bishops.

Another consideration would be additional forums and conferences, similar to
the Black Elk Convocation and Forum held at the University of Mary and the
North Dakota Heritage Center, with support of the North Dakota Humanities

Council, Native and non-Native scholars, and general community participants, were broad dialogue regarding cultural healing, which includes canonization ensue. In addition, continued, if not broadening support for Jacob's (2016) in-depth accounting of the Tekakwitha Conference, which has been an annual form for a broad array of indigenous cultural considerations, including canonization. Cultural consideration is key here, as Thiel and Vecsey (2012) drew attention to as "the most significant ways that American Indians can express their unique culture … by establishing and/or participating in a Kateri Circle at the parish where they attend." Kateri Circles are defined as a central source and force for the development of this initial by the Kateri Conference (website) as

> a group of Women and Men and/or Youth of all cultures within a parish/mission who want to belong to a prayer circle/group for the purpose of learning and promoting the saintly life of the Tekakwitha Conference patroness Kateri Tekakwitha…. (p. 51)

In additional consideration, continued context is critical regarding the tumultuous path established relative to the colonization of Christianity, when probing to understand the historically traumatic past in relation to triggering trauma of the present, and sadly future. Saints, whether indigenous or not, have their means to a particular historical end in consideration of canonization in the Catholic Church. When considering Kateri Tekakwitha, the recognition of her story and the cause for canonization spanned millennia. Interestingly, while she was "known and used over the centuries in Europe, the same was not so true in the U.S.," which is the origin of her life and death in 1680. Due to the migration of the missionaries to North America, Kateri's story was "kept alive," though at times the "impact dimmed for decades." It was until two hundred years after her death "the American Catholic Church had reason to resurrect Kateri's story," due to what the Church perceived as

> anti-Catholic and anti-immigrant forces of the late nineteenth century were battering the Church and its members. The Bishops looked for a symbol that was both Catholic and American to enhance its image. They found it in Kateri Tekakwitha. (Theil & Vecsey, 2012, p. 75)

This particular cause for canonization, coupled with more parochial evidence of advocacy as the bishops "were trying to make their Catholicism look truly American," was evident in missionary clergy who were boots on the ground like Francis M. Craft and Bishops Martin Marty and Shanley in the Great Plains, who promulgated a pastoral sense to Native people in consideration of Kateri Tekakwitha as a "patroness and example for The American Congregation, the sisterhood that he [Kraft] founded at Fort Yates, on the Standing Rock Reservation." Kraft also, among others like the Benedictines, approached education differently by apposing "the sending of Native children to distant boarding schools, thus angering school and government agents." Kraft's ministry notably did not end there, in fact, he was present and wounded at the Massacre of Wounded Knee, while trying to keep the peace, and also noted for his attempt to sustain the first ever order of Native American Sisters (Theil & Vecsey, 2012, p. 75).

And while many more venues and forums exist, to what end do they serve to perpetuate advancement in cultural healing as a synthesized, collective force is the question. Furthermore, could a monolith like the Catholic Church be such a place, along with its institutions of learning and partners to synthesize such dialogue with collective voices and literature? Again, context is critical when addressing contemporary challenges regarding the possibility of canonization that more earnestly is culturally responsive and relevant. This endeavor to embrace a cultural disposition toward canonization is undoubtedly both an opportunity and dilemma for the Catholic Church, both internal and external, for reasons previously explicated and additionally within this section of the chapter.

Jackson (2016) echoes this dilemma relative to the cause for sainthood and Native people with his depiction of writers painting Black Elk, for example, as "the old man as a bridge between the beliefs of the Old World and the New...." Further, Jackson described the cause for the sainthood of Kateri Tekakwitha as a process in which "not everyone is thrilled by the idea of sainthood: "...a Lakota woman working in the Catholic mission at the nearby Rosebud reservation flinched at the news ... She shook her head in disgust, but refused to say more...." And as Jackson notes, "Yet the process has already begun. Two documented 'miracles' are required by the Catholic Church to make someone a saint, and the search is under way (for Black Elk)" (p. 15).

Continual, pragmatism, if not healthy skepticism would seem to be warranted based on past precedence when considering cultural missteps within and outside of religious causes such as sainthood. MacCannell approaches such skepticism with his analysis of any case of an "ethnic group" selling itself in an image of itself or "museumized," where the local community "is forced in varying degrees to meet the tourists' expectations of what qualifies to be exotic" (as cited in Costello, 2005, p. 143). And with such a newer exposure of Native culture and spirituality misinterpreted with an expectation of what qualifies to be exotic, Kidwell et al. (2001) distilled even more preciously as issues with "control of sacred knowledge," which is "essential to the integrity of native religions." What is at stake relative to control of such knowledge is historically,

> Non-Indians have seized on this idea of esoteric knowledge to sell workshops and sweat lodges to people seeking spiritual enlightenment. Articulate political leaders are sometimes cited as sources of traditional knowledge, but they are generally not the custodians of tradition. Sacred knowledge resides in the elders who have heard the stories of previous generations. (p. 3)

So, with the benefit of stories of previous generations—and overall all the blunt history it has when shared from multiple cultural perspectives, with this sense of Black Elk speaking again—the critical point may be not as either saint or Lakota, but possibly both/and. Something Sweeney (2021) points out is, "Christians who are troubled by Black Elk's conversion seem to expect that he will disdain his Native background in ways that he clearly did not" (p. 78). And among other reasons articulated in this book, Kidwell et al. (2001) articulated well that, at its root of seeing one religious progress as solely binary, let alone Black Elk: "It is not reasonable to expect that any human being is ever able, consciously or not, to jettison all the cultural and spiritual baggage of experience" (Kidwell et al., 2001, p. 133).

Continual contemporary voices offered insights here with Black Elk's place historically as if at times as a wishbone being pulled among spiritual forces, both Native and non-Native. A force centered on questions such as that posed by Sweeney (2021) and answered by another contemporary voice (revisited from early portions of the book and critical to this portion) David Treuer (2019): "Was Black Elk a true Lakota in the second half of his life?" Many Indians prefer not to think about Black Elk's later years and consider his conversion as a kind of surrender, a confirmation that the old ways were in fact dead. Maybe, maybe not. Black Elk was determined to live and to adapt. That doesn't make him less of an Indian, as I see it; it makes him more of one (as cited in Sweeney, 2021, p. 86).

A point of "both/and" instead of "either/or" relative to Black Elk's determination to live and adapt making him not less of an Indian, but more of one, is additionally illuminated by Maka. When considering the impact of a newer story shared about Black Elk as a possible saint and those who may come again to his homeland areas as they did when inspired by *Black Elk Speaks,* Maka noted, "it'll be really important to start to make sense of where they're coming from and who's bringing them, and what's the relation there, and what learning are they getting or not getting. And then when they get here, what learning are they getting?" Plus, what "they" are learning and getting in relation to one another as again Native and non-Native people encounter one another around this person of Black Elk, there is a "potential" and "inevitability" for cultural healing to occur. However, again Maka offers a caution in terms of additional learning and "getting," on the way to such healing and discernment:

> The Lakota community is not a monolith, and so there will be people who deeply struggle with what will happen if he becomes a saint, there are people who will be deeply affirmed. There'll be people who just see it as another attempt at forced assimilation and just ongoing colonization. And all of the in-between, and I think it may just be a mixture of. So there will be diverse reaction, certainly from the Lakota community, just like there might be diverse reaction from the non-Lakota community. The problem I see, that I hope that can be different this time is, what the church didn't do with Saint Kateri, is it didn't engage in a deep conversation about the complexity of its history with indigenous peoples. We sort of all took it at face value, that this Mohawk woman was made a saint and there was nothing wrong with that, and that her story was unique and representative of the ease that native peoples in Catholicism have had. (Personal communication/interview, 2021–2022)

Summarily, within this complexity and tension inherent in a process of canonization of a Native American such as Kateri Tekakwitha, or Black Elk, or any future indigenous, for that matter, is what Reverend P. Michael Galvan said, at least for "Native Catholics" is a tension that "has been well documented in such classic works as *Black Elk Speaks, The Sacred Pipe and The Sixth Grandfather* to see the Lakota holy man's struggle...." Galvan continues:

> For many ... the tension between practicing the Native ways and the Catholic ways has been paramount. To deny either our Native or Catholic roots causes some identity confusion ... We need to remember that transformation, conversion, does not occur in relation to certain abstract principles, but in response to one's experiences and stories ... this conversion must take place within the context of their own experiences and stories. (as cited in Archambault et al., 2003, p. 209)

CHAPTER 5

Understanding Complex Stories of "A Certain Level of Mysticism"

Wičháȟpi Hiŋȟpaye (Fallen Star or Star Boy), the traditional hero of the Očhéthi Šakówiŋ, takes his place in the heavens with his father Wičháȟpi Owáŋžila (North Star).
© Dakota Goodhouse

The conversation regarding the complexity of history with indigenous peoples' own experiences and stories continues, and with anticipation carries forward a number of stories that have emerged within this book. As Thomas Merton keenly observed, what is needed for others to participate in this conversation about complexity and cultural healing is an understanding of "a certain level of mysticism…. like on a spiritual illumination beyond the ordinary conscious …" (As cited in Oldmeadow, 2018, p. 18).

While this illumination is not exclusive to any particular cultural group, it can be "taken for granted as normal part of life in an archaic culture," often missing an "essential component in the concept of a mature human personality" (p. 18). If anything can be gleaned from the stories shared, and scholars supported thoughts in this book, it would be the opportunity for more shared spiritual illumination, though perceived as separated by cultural barriers like language, often not separated by symbolic representations. As Holler (1995) observed:

> Freud decisively misunderstood the truth claims of religion,
> which are not the same logical type as scientific propositions,

but are instead symbolic. It would then be religion "means" in somewhat the same way as a work of art means—through the medium of culturally conditioned symbolic expression. (Holler, 1995, p. 216)

Included in what Holler constituted as symbolic, progress would be a form of communication not only bound in words, as Brown (2001) elaborated; rather, "silence itself constitutes language" for many Native cultures, and conversely for those of us in Western culture, there is often a "fear of silence...." Due to this fear of silence in Western culture, Brown postulated that "we do not let the power inherent in silence communicate with us ... [W]ithout silence, there cannot be language ... [and] in silence there are profound modes of sacred, humanizing communication." Furthermore, to remain consistent with the role Black Elk can play as a symbol both historically and today, he is known as sharing with Brown in translation, "Silence is the voice of the Great Mysterious" (p. 48).

Herein is the key to furthered dialogue and cultural healing, along with an understanding of the challenges associated with Native people relative to survivance, in terms of the medium of art and other forms of communication via silence, as a vehicle perpetuating intercultural symbolic expression and discernment. These steps toward the other in this vein are not one to take lightly, of course, because of cultural tensions today and accounts from those who have attempted such steps. Or, those in the midst of the process can quite possibly resonate with Fools Crow's testimony of Black Elk spending hours conversing with others such as priests, even in the wake of another priest who dismissed his healing practice, shared earlier in the book, as "devil begone!"

Holler (1995) offered that perhaps "Black Elk's susceptibility to religions went hand in hand with susceptibility to visions...." Meaning Black Elk's ability to perceive this synthesis of religions hand in hand with visions gave him the opportunity to promulgate "creative and courageous confrontations with Christianity and his engagement with the problems of his people make him so much more than simply a boy who fell sick and dreamed spectacularly of heaven." And as Holler commented further, this ability to confront other faith perspectives like Christianity with courage and creativity was and to many is symbolically represented in his life and work, which "embodies the best that was in his people and justifies his position as the greatest religious thinker yet produced by native North America" (Holler, 1995, pp. 220–221). A point by Holler that cannot be and that is supported by Oldmeadow (2018) as "salutary," meaning to remind ourselves that Black Elk did not "*create* his vision, he *received* it; he did not *author* the vision but only *transmitted* it...."

Oldmeadow (2018) astutely observed, "while a great deal of the recent scholarly discourse has obsessively focused on Black Elk and on Neihardt as individuals," collectively such discourse was "missing the overarching truth that each man was an instrument of larger forces which are not to be accounted for in the categories of 'biography' or of an impudent 'psychoanalysis'" (p. 71). Archambault (1998) described such a missing of the overarching truth accounted for in such stories as Oldmeadow (2018) referred to as "being ineffable," most likely due to story-shrouded "experiences" often cloaked from the Western imagination; therefore, begging such an imagination via "articulation" through "symbol and metaphor, through poem or story, or … whatever mode that one can utilize as a vehicle for expression." Coupled with what appears to be a primary example of others as a vehicle of expression is what Archambault identified as "Black Elk's conversion [to Catholicism] narrative seems to have been a product of this very personal, and very profound, experience" (p. 43).

Perspective is critical, in relation to the symbolic and the overarching truth, as Oldmeadow (2018) opined and Archambault (1998) described as ineffable, often only discernible through the articulation artistically of metaphor and symbol as a vehicle for expression. This articulation is significant while engaged in the complexity of the story and discernment among cultures. Black Elk's navigation and witness while doing so as a product of his times, according to Costello (2005), demonstrated the "reformulation of Lakota tradition [as] an expected product of economic [i.e., Great Depression] and demographic change…." In a religious context, Costello viewed Black Elk's navigating his times as one who "incorporated Christian thought into the Lakota cultural world … and use[d] … creativity to confront a changing world" (p. 90).

Within the rafts of research available on something as historically significant as a symbol of this developing thought, Holler (1995) pointed to the essential history of the Sun Dance "in modern times is its survival of change, repression, and neglect." And while such symbolic, spiritual expression was banned during the latter part of the 1800s, "the ban did not produce its intended result, the complete destruction of traditional belief and ritual…." Rather, Holler indicated that the attempt to destroy such a traditional belief and ritual "resulted in the present pluralistic situation, in which traditional religion coexists with a wide diversity of religious expression…." And while the intended result according to Holler, "has not been the hoped-for replacement of traditional religion with Christianity," the actual result may in fact be the "acceptance of both." Holler pointed to a sense of "bireligious" faithfulness among many Lakota who "profess belief in some form of denominational Christianity while continuing to practice traditional religion" (Holler, 1995, pp. 202–203).

And whether perspectives shared here may see this sense of bireligiousness as the end product of forced assimilation over centuries of colonization, or a more natural, spiritual progression to both forms of spiritual practice embodied in the Sun Dance. A progression as Holler (1995) highlighted is a synthesis of traditional and Christian communities. A highlighted view that is hard to argue is the present-day existence of Native people like the Lakota whose spiritual practice was to be fully replaced, if not also the people themselves via genocide-like tactics. This sense of bireligiousness would seem to speak to what Archambault (1998) noted in the person of Black Elk, a prime example of "the resiliency of Black Elk's spiritual genius…." Along with this genius, Archambault refers to the resiliency of "his people," who "had been pushed violently into a historic period for which there was no comparison, no reference point to prepare them for such catastrophic changes." Moreover, what seems to escape the consciousness of most who profess to be in touch with history is that "almost overnight their free, nomadic, self-directed existence became a life hedged in geographically, restricted at every level to the confines of the reservation … he served as a healer among his people in those early reservation years…." And in this overnight change, Maka called an exceptional people, Black Elk, with all the accolades of a significant healer among his people, was not exempt from this dark history of the near extinction of an honorable people and was in fact "part of the generation forced 'to create their own patterns of behavior'" (p. 25).

Finally, before concluding this book by examining the implications of Black Elk's life speaking "that much … more" in terms of present-day challenges associated with Native people and survivance, DeMallie (1984) summarizes this chapter well, noting that "the far-reaching influence that Black Elk's teachings have on the idea and attitudes of countless individuals today are," for Indians and non-Indians…." And how such teaching testifies "to basic religious and philosophical dilemmas generated by a sense of increasing alienation from the natural world." This reflection on alienation from the natural world cannot be overemphasized, as it is not exclusive to the Indigenous peoples of North America. Similar issues have arisen and continue their challenges in places like Ireland, where the Irish are also in the process of decolonization, striving to retrieve their spiritual roots grounded in the Divine while also rooted in the natural world (Taylor, 2022).

As DeMallie (1984) articulated further, while Black Elk is what Maka called earlier in the book a "paragon" for his Lakota people, for instance, and "for many, Black Elk suggests a perspective on a prior, more satisfying relations between man and nature." Still for others, "his teachings are a blueprint for religious revitalization" (p. 80). Internationally, this phenomenon would hold to be true as witnessed by the revival of *Black Elk Speaks* due to C.G. Jung and others who discovered his mystical writings. Closer to home, "Black Elk's teachings appear to be evolving into consensual American Indian theological canon …" (p. 80). Within the formation of such a consensual canon, DeMallie presented critical questions to not only be further discerned and facilitated by dialogue throughout a variety of communities of learning but also within the final portion of this book, by means of summative implications, with the intent of not falling into the trap of what DeMallie called a dialogue that "usually dissolves into political rhetoric rather than objective assessment" (p. 80).

Let us not fall into the trap of rhetoric or even the blindness associated with the sterile Petrie dish–like missteps associated with objective assessment-run amok. Let's approach the following questions and the implications considered in the final part of this book, as paragons in our own humble way considering the stories told here and many more to come as culture unfolds in an intercultural way:

> What is Black Elk's place in the history of Lakota religion? Does he truly represent the old Lakota way, or history of Lakota religion? Does he truly represent the old Lakota way, or was his thinking profoundly affected by Catholicism? (DeMallie, 1984, p. 80)

CONCLUSION

Sam Wagner/Shutterstock.com

Black Elk's Life Speaks: "That Much ... More" As ...

This book concludes by examining the implications of Black Elk's life speaking "that much ... more." There are stories, mindful of DeMallie's (1984) latter questions posed as a subtext, that bring forward the primary areas of the paper into concluding areas in which Black Elk's life may be speaking: first, this book will examine Black Elk's life speaking as an educator particular, and from the field of education at large; second, as culture bearers; third, as a model of and for survivance; and fourth, and finally, the implications of the life of Black Elk's life speaking "that much ... more" as an "Old Man," and his dreams and visions yesterday, today, and beyond.

... EDUCATOR AND EDUCATION

As an educator who strives to be a social constructivist, I am always hoping to build knowledge collectively within a community of learners, often echoing the seminal works of models such as John Henry Newman, Parker Palmer, and Padraig Pearce. Black Elk would be a recent addition to the list, primarily because like Irish education activist Pearce, he seemed to model a return to culture at its most natural essence as the first step into a broader world with feet firmly planted in cultural self-identity (Taylor, 2022).

Strikingly, the latter examples of cultural identity, while in their own right profound, historically seem to be very keenly aware of one another's challenges associated with this quest for identity while peeling back layers of colonization. Black Elk's son Ben, along with others, made note of this, commenting, "I found out that European people know more about us Indians than people in the States. They study us ... our culture ... history right from the start, from the schools. Well, we don't here" (DeSersa et al., 2000, p. 21). The sense of "we" here is important, as often this is intended on a systemic level in terms of cultural awareness, which is often led by the academy or institutions of higher learning.

Accordingly, if Ben Black Elk's perception is still accurate, and it may not be too much of a risk to assume so, then possibly Taiaiake Alfred's thoughts of "indigenizing the academy" as a move to bring about change in universities so that they, along with society at large, can "become places where values, principles and modes of organization and behavior of our people are respected in." Further, Alfred opined that the possibility of such change would include a process of integration "into the larger system of structures and processes that make up the university ..." Indigenous researcher Twiss takes Alfred's call to action personally, and I would imagine more broadly in the academy, to come into confrontation with the fact that universities are intolerant of and resistant to meaningful indigenizing ... our experiences in universities reflect the tensions and dynamics of our relationships as Indigenous peoples interacting with people and institutions in society as a whole; an existence of constant and pervasive struggle to resist assimilation to the values and culture of the larger society....

Similar to sharing Twiss's commitment to Alfred's invitation overall, it would appear the implications for educators and education would be more akin to a particular vocational call, meaning to work "to ensure the survival of our culture and nations," as we pursue higher education for future generations as a means of creating a collaborative independence as coinhabitants in the land and establishing our places in the modern world" (as cited in Twiss, 2015, pp. 58–59).

Generally, Alfred's call and Twiss's (2015) affirmation, along with other scholars' call to action, reflect in a broad meaning Black Elk's life has spoken and continues to speak. Insofar as how Black Elk's life speaks today, it would appear his life can speak to a serious scholarly critique and cautionary dialogue, according to Costello (2005), as "rereading a contemporary position of Lakota society back into history is questionable scholarship." Questionable indeed, and this is why cultural models of education such as Black Elk symbolically and Twiss, Alfred, and Costello today, among others, should be the basis for such scholarly critique before doing what Costello fears:

> privileging the interpretations of cultural outsiders as more accurate and valuable that those living and creating the culture is anthropological discrimination that completely disregards Lakota communal memory, destroys their agency, and borders on racism. (p. 71)

It is strong language indeed captured by Costello (2005), but in reality, based on the stories shared in this book, without those voices of narrative resistance "anthropological discrimination" persists. Even as such discrimination chips away at agency, bordering on racism, there are opportunities for narrative resistance to prevail with a developing indigenous-based and ally scholarship, who hold central to the role stories shared here and countless others, adding to the tremendous, cavernous gap that pervades in the body of culture research.

Again, Black Elk's life enters, as one that has run the risk of disregard as Costello (2005) mentioned in general and has been known to also develop in the more recent history of Black Elk's account as a Catholic, of which Costello viewed as "real as any other part of his life and cannot be separated from his Lakota world. The 'gap' between Indigenous American culture and Christianity is not a part of Black Elk's Lakota worldview, but merely a reflection of modern academic bias" (p. 71). This may push the envelope with those who may have followed this section in terms of disregarding agency or bordering, if not outright racism when it comes to representing Native culture. However, bias in the context, Costello asserted, is important within the entire constellation of scholarship on Black Elk as a critical beacon addressing such challenges with cultural accuracy and agency. Frankly, without the more recent scholarship by Costello, Steltenkamp, Jackson, and so on, Black Elk may not even be a factor in such dialogue within and beyond the academy, which would be sorely missed and potentially a setback in terms of cultural healing. The academy does have a role to play in cultural healing if scholars are willing to address modern academic bias and research gaps between Native American culture and Christianity. Consequently, academicians' own reticence regarding Christianity should not deny the opportunity for cultural healing.

At its best, the academy and other allies have an opportunity to bring all voices to the fore and dignify all voices, most notably indigenous, in the process of cultural healing. At its worst, the academy can risk self-subjugation to irreversibility or dominance of thought. Palmer (1998) postulated that such thought happens in an academic culture when we are surprised by a new idea that does not fit our conventional frame … in a flattened, desacralized culture, thinking is not what happens when we are taken—or threatened—by surprise … we reflexively defend ourselves…. [with] an old idea, a _conceptual club_ (underline and italics for effect) can beat the surprise to death—or run away before it makes a mark on our minds. (pp. 112–113)

Hopefully and optimistically, considering the academy at its best, all academic and other parties involved in such healing would acquire what Holler (1995) identified, as a result of his work with the Lakota in particular, a "perspectival shift in my philosophical thinking, something the anthropologists call 'acquiring a cross-cultural perspective'…" Holler further articulated best what I tried to encapsulate regarding Costello's (2005) thoughts about modern academic bias when Holler confessed,

We humanists have mostly ignored the religion of technologically primitive cultures, perhaps because of an uncritical tendency to equate primitive technology with primitive thought … [N]ative North America is a fascinating study that casts new light on religious change and adaptation … [M]y encounter with Native North America has been the greatest intellectual challenge and adventure of my adult life. I recommend a similar encounter highly to those of my colleagues in the humanities who have ears to hear, for this is an endeavor that greatly repays serious thought. (p. xviii)

Holler offers key thoughts to ponder for the academy far and near and beyond, as the implications of his recommendation should be strongly considered based on his modeling and that of other academics who have actually invested time with other cultures in order to come to such profound thoughts as those expressed above.

These thoughts and serious academic studies, by the way, lead ultimately to a change in manner and delivery for both educators and education. As Owens (1998) pointed out through the enlistment of Luther Standing Bear, the realization of such serious thought is not devoid or empty in this world. If we fail to engage with it and neglect to

create it … not only does our environment become more fragile, but we are forever cut off from a part of our inheritance as living beings in a richly interconnected web of life. We must learn to ask the trees and stones for permission to take them into our lives for our survival, and we have to lay ourselves close to the earth for a long, patient time in order, along with N. Scott Momaday's grandfather, actually to see the powerful reality that is before us and part of us. Such closeness of vision, reciprocity, and respect are powerful medicines, the only ... that may ... save humanity from itself. This is a lesson Native Americans and all indigenous peoples really do have to teach, and it is time the world began to listen carefully. (p. 236)

A vision, no doubt, accords with Black Elk, along with other Native Americans and Indigenous peoples in general, along with those outside looking in. These exemplars are best positioned to save humanity from itself, based on an educational credo to share this vision of reciprocity and respect as a powerful medicine, with an invitation and call to the world to listen carefully.

Once more, this may come as news to some from the outside looking in, as some may feel they are charged with this responsibility to save humanity, yet as Owens (1998) shares, what is novel today is a growing recognition of the subversive survival of Indigenous Americans.

Five hundred years after Columbus' first voyage, this survival is being illuminated in the United States through a proliferating body of literature by Native Americans demonstrating the "Discoverer" succeeded beyond his more earnest expectations ... Native Americans are ensuring, as Robert Young has written, "...the First World is now having to come to terms with the fact that it is no longer always positioned in the first person with regard to be Second or Third Worlds" ... Native Americans are beginning ... to demand that non-Indian readers acknowledge differing epistemologies ... across a new "conceptual horizon," and learn to read in new ways. (Owens, 1998, p. 4)

In summary, relative to Black Elk's life speaking as an educator and in education, there is this sense of him speaking to Native Americans in terms of Owens' (1998) clarion call, in the face of an academic emergence, for others to acknowledge and dignify profound thoughts and belief spiritually, and across a horizon. This horizon is only perceived as new, frankly because, after centuries of oppression, the resiliency of Native people has persevered and returned perceptively to others as new. Yet, in reality, it is only unfamiliar to those "non-Indian" and is now "beginning" to be in concert with other cultures. Most likely, as Owens (1998) commented, Native Americans, and all Indigenous peoples, are embodied as culture bearers, like Black Elk, and will have to teach (again) in order to save humanity from itself (again).

...CULTURE BEARER

Black Elk's life speaking, as a culture bearer, would appear to be replete historically in a number of given contexts. Furthermore, when considering those contexts in relation to today, it is often similar to what many Native Americans tend to share; as Anton Treuer (2012/2021) has been known to state, "Indians we are so often imagined, but so infrequently well understood" (p. 1). Or, as some would contend, "we are still here," as if the romanticized view of Native Americans has taken over the fact that millions are still not only surviving in North America for that matter but, in a sense, thriving in a number of demographic categories (D. Treuer, 2019).

This perceived paradox of perception, and reality relative to Native American active presence, along with the way in which Black Elk speaks as a cultural and spiritual bearer, tends to gravitate to Deloria's (1944) expressed seminal thoughts regarding the appearance that the quest to discern what lies hidden in the past may be of interest "to be sure." He affirmed the fact that Native people are still here today, and Black Elk's life still speaks, connects with Deloria's focused thoughts that the past is "not so important as the present and the future. The vital concern is not where a people came from, physically, but where they are going spiritually" (cited in Jacobs, 2008, p. 136).

Further, in the milieu of where Black Elk's life speaks as a culture bearer, Steltenkamp (1993) pinpointed this direction in terms of his life going "beyond the neat construct of total nativism ... or complete absorption of Western ways...." Additionally, in terms of the biographical nature of Black Elk, Steltenkamp boldly stated that such nature is not a "profile in syncretism ... rather an example of reflexive adjustment to new cultural landscapes that previously have not been explored" (p. xxi). This statement, to those not impacted by the comment on syncretism is bold, due to those who seem to advocate for syncretism as if the outdated concept of melting pot—or more directly forced assimilation—has merit. Steltenkamp illumined this point further by holding that Black Elk symbolically and spiritually was (and I would add "is") "neither an artifactual relic of the bison-hunting era, nor was he a prisoner to its substance, even though much literature and opinion suggest this was the case—for him and most others" (p. 148).

All being well, breaking the shackles of binary thinking that would isolate the person of Black Elk historically, culturally, and spiritually would permit a more holistic view of Black Elk contextually. According to Archambault (1998), more appropriately "Black Elk is a culture bearer," which is a more inclusive descriptor of Black Elk,

> means he embodied and enacted values which led to a spiritual transformation and cultural change … described as "… individuals who … are deeply transparent to the Holy Spirit [Wakan–Tanka] and give voice to ideas that express the loving will of the Spirit for humankind as a whole." (p. 93)

Bolstering Archambault's description of Black Elk as a culture bearer, Jesuit writer Paul Manhart brought a helpful image to what this description looks like metaphorically as someone who fitted [and still fits] "cultures together like a puzzle and thus neither was dissolved" (As cited in DeSersa et al., 2000, p. xv). This is a helpful image, considering that all the puzzle pieces, while distinctive as cultures are, together represent a mosaic of cultures that collectively can represent an image of expressed affinity, in contrast with dated metaphors of assimilation (Taylor, 2022). Those with religious vocations, like Jesuit Manhart and others, tend to lend helpful imagery when navigating the often parochial, troubled waters in a spiritual context.

Kempis (1999) shed further light on the navigation of such waters with an example posited of missionaries, and why many Jesuit Catholic missionaries, though not without scrutiny in their missionary history, did find resonance with a culture bearer like Black Elk. This resonates due to their belief that Native people felt alienated, as if "strangers to the world but close and familiar to God." Further, Kempis shared their self-perception that although "this present world saw them as contemptible, in the eyes of God they were precious and beloved." And due to this grounding in "true humility, lived in simple obedience, and walked in love and patience," Native people "profited daily in the spirit and obtained great grace in God's sight." And possibly, not solely in God's sight, as Kempis further notes, for indigenous believers serve as an example spiritually

> to all religious people, and they should stimulate us to strive for spiritual excellence far more than all those who live lukewarm lives should tempt us to be lax … Their footsteps still remain to testify that they were indeed holy and perfect people who fought valiantly and trod the world under their feet. (Kempis, 1999, pp. 52–53)

Thus, to recapitulate, Black Elk's speaking as a culture bearer, with the example of footsteps remaining to be followed by all religious people, stories enter into the fabric of importance when discerning the relevancy of Black Elk's life speaking. Speaking, as Costello (2005) underscored in his careful consideration of Neihardt's encounter with Black Elk and stories shared. Black Elk, according to Costello, "shaped his story for his audience, not deceiving or being dishonest, but sincerely telling about those aspects of his life in which Neihardt was interested." And with this earnest approach to imparting Native wisdom and understanding, Costello also enlisted another familiar author, Louis Owens, who described this phenomenon of story being shaped for various audiences as a

> Mask ... realized over centuries through Euro-America's construction of the Indian Other ... to be recognized, and to have a voice that is heard by those in control of power, the Native must step into the mask and be the Indian constructed by white America. Paradoxically, like the mirror, the mask merely shows the Euro-American to himself, since the Native [remains] behind the mask unseen, unrecognized ... While the historical and cultural dynamics limited an accurate sharing and later telling of Black Elk's sacred vision, Neihardt enabled Black Elk's vision to survive. (as cited in Costello, 2005, pp. 155–157)

Whereas Neihardt will be revisited as this book comes to a formal close, Owens forecasts well the close to the book, as he articulated a key point regarding the central, seminal role Neihardt (1932/1971) played in terms of Black Elk's speaking at the time of his interviews, and then through countless editions of *Black Elk Speaks*. Neihardt's interviews and assessments remain equally critical today as Black Elk speaks through this book, and among throngs of generations. Generations including Native Americans, who have various cultural roles like a culture bearer, with Black Elk's life speaking, look to others, and are looked at, as models of and for survivance in the face of a landscape desperately fighting to retain the last vestiges of colonialism.

... MODEL OF AND FOR SURVIVANCE

Regarding Black Elk's life speaking as a model of and for survivance, Jackson (2016), whose blunt analysis seems to be devoid of partiality, encapsulated well this relation of Black Elk and survivance today, particularly at times, as it builds on the previous focused section on Black Elk as a culture bearer.

To that end, Jackson (2016) noted the difficulty of carving out a particular brand of spiritual worship among Native American people whose "religion often does not orbit around a church, can be as diverse as the nation's 567 legally recognized tribes or its 5.22 million half and full-blood individuals." Interestingly, Jackson enlisted one of the primary "fathers" of the boarding schools, "Richard Henry Pratt, who said, 'made the Indian, Indian,'" in terms of identifying what spiritual worship aligns with what tribe. This is also akin to understanding the development of the term *survivance*, which Jackson attributed to "Native American intellectuals," who coined a "cold and distant word for a struggle waged on the black road ... here on the Great Plains one can feel the relentless grind of history...." As stark as this struggle has been, Jackson painted a light at the end of the tunnel, with Black Elk as a model of survivance and whose speaking life "lay at the heart of this resurgence when he chose to save the ancient ways." And even in this light as the heart of resurgence, Black Elk did express despondence, as any model of survivance would be permitted, as "every path threw up another obstacle, and too often he thought he'd failed" (p. 483). Some may see this perspective as not ideal for a model of survivance, yet others have also portrayed their "dark night of the soul" experiences that have been helpful to many in times of travail—so why would Black Elk's expression of humanity be denied?

Additional context is most likely warranted when considering such a mystical, spiritual abyss, and personal interior darkness, as the "dark night of the soul." Regarding the tradition of mysticism within Christian circles, Catholic, for example, this journey in and through spiritual darkness is "nothing new" according to editor and commentator Brian Kolodiejchuk (2007), whose work focused on the private writings of Mother Teresa joining the company of mystics who struggled spiritually in interior darkness. As an exemplar mystic, and eventually canonized saint by the Catholic Church, who to the surprise of most who globally venerated her, Mother Teresa penned in her private writings, "If I ever I become a Saint—I will surely be one of darkness. I will continually be absent from Heaven—to light the light of those in darkness on earth ..." (pp. 1–2).

With Mother Teresa as an exemplar guiding his work, Kolodiejchuk (2007) commented further—this struggle with interior darkness spiritually—"it has been a common phenomenon among numerous saints throughout Church history who have experienced what the Spanish Carmelite mystic St. John of the Cross termed the 'dark night.'" Adding more intricacy and intensity to this mystical are "two phases: the 'night of the senses,'" where God still "communicates His light and love" (pp. 22–23).

Nevertheless, the mystic's soul, "imperfect as it is, is incapable of receiving" God's communication, and experiences such communication "as darkness, pain, dryness, and emptiness. Although the emptiness and absence of God are only apparent, they are a great source of suffering ... Though consolations are no longer felt, there is a notable longing for God, and an increase of love, humility, patience, and other virtues." With this first phase, also known as the "first night," the experience of this night is often a segue, "led by God into the 'night of the spirit,' to be purged from the deeper roots of one's imperfections ... A state of extreme aridity ... one feels rejected and abandoned by God ... Prayer is difficult, almost impossible, spiritual counsel practically of no avail; and various external trials may add to this pain." Despite this dire stage of the phase of "the night of the spirit," there is means to an end in terms of this phase's "pain purification," as the mystic is "led to total detachment from all created things and to a lofty degree of union with Christ, become a fit instrument in His hands and serving Him purely and disinterestedly" (Kolodiejchuk, 2007, pp. 22–23).

A return to Mother Teresa as a specific exemplar and either established exemplar in this arduous process of traversing the darkest of the dark reaches of spiritual, mystical exodus from superfluous light many others tend to bask in. Again, forecasting to the close of this book and the similar fashion in which Black Elk traverses the phases of nights embodied in sense and spirit, Mother Teresa demonstrated again, in her own hand, her own dark night of the soul as:

> terrible darkness ... this continual longing for God—which gives me pain deep in my heart ... Darkness is such that I really do not see—neither with my mind nor with my reason. The place of God in my soul is blank ... There is no God in me ... When the pain of longing is so great ... He does not want me ... He is not there ... God does not want me ... Sometimes I just hear my own heart cry out "My God," and nothing else comes ... This torture and pain I can't explain. (Kolodiejchuk, 2007, pp. 1–2)

Mystics such as Saints Mother Teresa and John of the Cross, among others, are the company Black Elk has held, and I would submit still holds today, as his voice speaks at large, particularly under often the historically traumatic weight in the process and path of and for survivance.

Further context is constructive here, along with Jackson's (2016) consistent candor, in recounting the mind of Black Elk as he chose to bear cultural responsibility for his Lakota people and even "for all nations, even his enemy," as he wrestled with "his choice though he always wondered if he'd choose wisely." Once more, considering Black Elk wrestling with the wisdom of choice, this sense of a "dark night of the soul" returns and thereby brings forth even more inspirational humanity of Black

Elk, most intensely exemplified in his direct experience with the 1890 Massacre at Wounded Knee leading to an emotion of "hatred" due to his desire to "die with them, but it was not to be" (pp. 332–333).

"To the end of his life," via Neihardt's interview accounts, "Black Elk would never think that he'd done enough to save his people," as he struggled with vivid, mental "pictures of the dead [that] would not go away." These vivid, mental pictures held for years by Black Elk regarding Wounded Knee were eventually shared in more graphic detail, thus giving more perspective to the trauma, depicted as: "bodies lay in heaps; sometimes, scattered down a ravine. Sometimes bunches of them had been killed and torn to pieces where the wagon guns hit them. I saw a little baby trying to touch its mother, but she was bloody and dead" (Jackson, 2016, pp. 332–333). With regret and consternation embodied in Black Elk is the torment of his soul aforementioned, questions pondered by Jackson, may have very likely been pondered by Black Elk himself: "What if he'd used his power? Would it have saved the slaughtered and innocent?" Pointedly again, Jackson gets to the heart of why Black Elk's life is a model for and of survivance, in reference to this experience of trauma impacting even those who are models among models, because along with their perceived glory as models, also comes their humanity, for "even those we call holy can dream of revenge" (pp. 332–333).

Thus, in the stories of Black Elk that have unfolded throughout this book, and those most recently embodied in his ultimate questioning of what real purpose his life may have served (particularly in the face of a calamity like Wounded Knee), is what Vizenor (2008) identified: survivance as "invariably true and just in native practice and company …," because similarly, it is "unmistakable in native stories, natural reason, remembrance, traditions, and customs and is clearly observable in narrative resistance and personal attributes…." And again, with the model of Black Elk's life speaking to and for survivance, in addition, it speaks to the overall:

> character of survivance and how this creates a sense of native presence over absence, nihility, and victimity … [It] is an active sense of presence over absence and oblivion … [It] is the continuance of stories, not a mere reaction, however pertinent … [and] is greater than the right of a survivable name … The practices of survivance create an active presence, more than the instincts of survival, function, or subsistence. (pp. 1, 11)

An important distinction posited by Vizenor (2008), in terms of the practice of survivance superseding the instinct for survival, function, or subsistence, which speaks directly to the imperative of Black Elk's speaking "that much … more" by means of the composite of stories shared in this book. This is the active presence Vizenor pointed to, along with the adherence to the continuance of stories; and, as Roger also addressed as an aspect of active presence, the critical cognizance of language as the foundation of culture, linking "cultural knowledge to the survival of people." Specifically, he alluded to remembering "the traditions and generations." Roger cautioned, without such remembering, "current generations would simply not be here without the knowledge, wisdom and teachings of the past generations" (as cited in Jacob, 2013, p. 57).

... "OLD MAN": DREAM/VISION YESTERDAY, TODAY, AND BEYOND

The final section, very much in consideration of Roger's previous caution "without such remembering...," in an exploration of the implications of Black Elk's life speaking as the "Old Man" with, remembering dreams and of yesterday, today, and beyond.

For those who revel in the weeds of research, or even just a good book that takes one to unexpected places approaching a climax that borders on ecstasy, I share a similar experience while writing this book. I never intended, in exploring the implications of Black Elk's life speaking "that much ... more," to end up essentially at the start with John Neihardt's (1932/1971) interviews of Black Elk. My intention was to explore the more contemporary sense of how Black Elk's life may speak today via his descendants, as the word to date on Black Elk. A nuanced sense of Black Elk speaking, I do believe has been established, and most likely with great anticipation, will continue to be developed beyond the scope of this book.

Accordingly, with all the voices that have spoken concerning Black Elk, Black Elk himself, descendants, Native and non-Native scholars, and others, I had thought it would lead me further from Neihardt's (1932/1971), and even Brown's (1971), follow-up in the twilight of Black Elk's life. Nevertheless, it will be these two who will synthesize—ironically, and even paradoxically enough—the final word regarding Black Elk's life speaking. Speaking in the context of Neidhart's affinity for Black Elk's "old man," with expressed dreams and visions, that I assert collectively demonstrates Black Elk's life speaking "that much ... more" yesterday, today, and beyond.

I have hiked what today is Black Elk's Peak, in the Black Hills, several times in the past few years, since I have been awakened by the tremendous way in which Black

Elk's life speaks relative to the tremendous impact Native American culture can have in terms of deepening the sense of place spiritually for those still here, and those who have come. Hence, when Neihardt (1932/1971) shared his climatic communion with Black Elk on previously named Harney's Peak, as an echo of the colonial impact of what Maka called his Lakota people as "exceptional," I could indeed feel and see the geography of this Peak, which at 7,000 feet stands above any other in the present-day state of South Dakota.

This vision was clearer to me as others Neihardt has painted in terms of the geography, overall and more pointedly, Black Elk's domicile in the Manderson area of the Pine Ridge Reservation, along with his birthplace at the confluence of the Little Powder and Powder Rivers near the board of Wyoming and Montana. A stunning place, who's location was first shared to me by an emerging Native scholar Dakota Goodhouse (2019, 2020), whose scholarship has opened up vast fields of Native geographic and spiritual discernment. The impact of such scholarship personally, and I would submit in certain circles of Black Elk related scholarship in particular, has given pause for scholars most often non-Native to reconsider broader, holistic ways in which phenomenon can be viewed beyond what some would call a Settler or Western European view. An example of this would be Goodhouse's plethora of seminal works highlighting the People of Seven Council Fires or the *Ochetchi Sakowin*. Notable among the works, the traditional hero Fallen Star or Star Boy who, in celestial fashion, takes his place in the heavens with his father, the North Star. Fallen Star was known by the People as "the Protector, the bringer of light and higher consciousness." After becoming a father, Fallen Star ascended "a hill at night with a friend" and told him he was going to return home, and subsequently laid down on the hilltop and died. His spirit was seen as a light that rose into the star world and "at some point in the past, all *Lakota* acquired the gift of light he brought to them." While this story shared an encapsulated account and thereby carries greater contextual complexity, what is evident is the striking significance in terms of what most likely prefigures how most Christians would identify this account as the celestial cue leading astrologers to Jesus. Confounding to some in terms of this prefigured nature, yet incredibly enlightening to others in terms of scholarship, if not reorientating one's spiritual, dare say, religious focus. Given serious consideration, to what I would identify as Native or Indigenous spiritual geography, this is yet another portal to ways in which Black Elk's life speaks "that much…more." As a result, geography is vivid and discernable when Black Elk via Neihardt speaks; nevertheless, when it comes to dreams and visions expressed, this is more complex in terms of affiliation. And maybe that is the point, like the "dark night of the soul" experiences shared earlier when considering the implications of Black Elk speaking as a culture bearer.

Undoubtedly, Black Elk's gift to Native and non-Native people, while not necessarily alike, is the opportunity to share in his lament and at the same time triumph of the active presence of survivance over the "victimity" of survival, as was highlighted earlier by Vizenor (2008). Even amid the depiction Neihardt (1932/1971) paints of the Peak itself when Black Elk reflected on his life as "black above the far sky rim," the reflection began distinctively, yet possibly common to those most rooted in one's culture spiritually with a vision of spirits taking Black Elk "to the center of the earth [to] show me all good things in the sacred hoop of the world." This reminds me of C.S. Lewis's Irish roots taking him to an ancient grounding of pure joy in his autobiography *Surprised by Joy* (Taylor, 2022), particularly when Black Elk referred to his spiritually blissful moment and the hope to stay in that bliss, as Neihardt recounted,

> I wish I could stand up there in the flesh before I die, for there is something I want to say to the Six Grandfathers … (to his son Ben) … If I have any power left, the thunder beings of the west should hear me when I send a voice, and there should be at least a little thunder and a little rain…. (pp. 231–234)

Neihardt (1932/1971) described further the contrast of these beatific-like moments with a day bright and cloudless, though in a season of drought—in fact, "one of the worst in the memory of the old man …" And with the "old man," as this unfolds for the two, Neihardt shared how they "listened now, noted that the thin clouds had gathered around us. A scant chill rain began to fall and there was low, muttering thunder without lightening…." Notable here is how silence is the forebearer of discernment. This is significant and resonates for me as an author and otherwise, as I contemplate and discern a Benedictine, monastic-like call to serve in Christ as an oblate, prioritized with a "good zeal," and the initial word of the Rule of Benedict, "listen." A period of listening is what Neihardt shared, as he witnesses the twilight of this seminal Lakota healer: "for some minutes the old man stood silent, with face uplifted, weeping in the drizzling rain. In a little while the sky was clear again" (Neihardt, 1932/1971, pp. 231–234).

One can only pause, and if one resonates enough with this moment shared intimately, and vicariously for the rest of us, maybe this is inherent in at least the non-Native speculation of Neihardt's (1932/1971) account—could it be envy? I will admit such inclination toward envy at times maybe less so now. Yet, the words are still here and so are those who bear this culture sustained by this poet from Nebraska, which may be the point of it all, as has also been mentioned in so many words earlier. Neihardt modeled his own transformation to a broader sense of cultural awareness as he admitted, "It was not information that was lacking for my purpose ... What I needed for my purpose was something to be experienced through intimate contact, rather than received through telling...." This is a significant admission by Neihardt, which is critical modeling for me, and I would suspect other scholars who walk the tightrope of intercultural understanding. What is more, it would appear with this awareness that Neihardt models the responsibility of being cognizant of the spiritual depths, if not "sacred obligation," that he not only felt per se but more deeply felt "to be true to the old man's meaning and manner of expression," that Neihardt was convinced "there were times when we had more than ordinary means of communication" (pp. 231–234).

The layers of modeling witnessed in terms of Black Elk's life speak directly via the life, and words of John Neihardt (1932/1971) is a significant example—significant most likely due to random circumstances or maybe synchronicity, leading to the impact of Black Elk's life speaking to someone whose original scholarship was not intended to be rooted within the cultural realm of a Lakota healer. Neihardt's words and admonition seemed to have clarified this rendezvous of poet and healer:

> for the last forty years it has been my purpose to bring Black Elk's message to the white world as he wished me to do ... The general public, with practically no knowledge of Indians, gave it a very modest reception ... A generation passed, but the book refused to die. Somehow a copy found its way to Zurich, Switzerland and was appreciated by a group of German scholars, including the late Carl Jung ... The news of the book reached America and found some friendly appreciators ... it became "the current youth classic," (and with TV exposure) ... exploded into surprising popularity ... spreading throughout the US and Europe, having been translated into eight languages. The old prophet's wish that I bring his message to the world is actually being fulfilled ... Perhaps with this message spreading across the world he has not failed. (Neihardt, 1932/1971, pp. ix–xii)

Perhaps this very book, along with other current dialogue regarding the potential of Black Elk's canonization, would be further evidence to support Neihardt's (1932/1971) last sentence above. Along with his successor Joseph Epes Brown, who encountered Black Elk at the very twilight of his life until his death, thereby carrying the torch of not only particular scholarship about this Lakota healer but also in witness of the direct personal impact that intercultural relations can have in a more vulnerable and overall authentic way.

Brown (1971) reflected pointedly on the last time Black Elk had literally spoken, regarding the changes that must take place and the "new perspective and in a new light" that Black Elk speaks to a modern world. At the time, according to Brown, Black Elk was lamenting the "broken hoop of his nation, it was ... to be only a matter of time before the Indians with their seemingly archaic and anachronistic cultures would be completely assimilated into a larger American society convinced of its own superiority and the validity of its goals." Toward this concern regarding assimilation Brown comments, "we still are far from being aware of the dimensions and ramifications of our ethnocentric illusions...." And though challenging, to climb out of such an impact of assimilation, Brown offered a possible constructive process of

> intense self-examination and to engage in a serious reevaluation of the premises and orientations of our society ... almost all Indian groups that retain any degree of self-identity are now reevaluating, and giving positive valuation to, the fundamental premise of their own traditional cultures.... (pp. xv–xvi)

Since Brown's (1971) thoughts were expressed decades ago, whether his analysis and ties to Black Elk hold relevance today, or in his words "if there is validity," Brown said that it may be premature to speculate on the impact of Black Elk's mission to "bring people back to 'the good red road,'" or even if Black Elk "failed as he thought it had." Another critical perspective shared by Brown, and inherent in the overall thrust of this book in the way that Black Elk's life speaks "that much ... more," is "his mission may be succeeding in ways he could not have anticipated" (Brown, 1971, pp. xv–xvi).

What remains to be seen is, in the face of historical trauma, survivance, and cultural healing, how Black Elk's life continues to impactfully speak through additional familial, and related stories, as the educator, culture bearer, and "old man" dreamer and visionary, he is and continues to be for time in perpetuity.

References

America Magazine. (2022, June 25). Pope Francis' Apology to the Indigenous Peoples in Canada (Full text). *America: The Jesuit Review.* https://www.americamagazine.org/

Archambault, M. T. (1998). *Black Elk: Living in the sacred hoop.* Saint Anthony Messenger Press.

Archambault, M. T., Thiel, M. G., & Vecsey, C. (2003). *The crossing of two roads: Being catholic and native in the United States.* Orbis Books.

Bears, B., Berdache, B., & Beings, B. (2020). *Contrary Native Other.* Amazon.com.

Black Elk, M. (June 3, 2021, August 17, 2021). Interview with Black Elk Great, Great, GreatGrandson Maka Black Elk. (Taylor, M. W., Interviewer)

Black Elk, W., & Lyon, W. S. (1991). *Black Elk: The sacred ways of a Lakota.* HarperSanFrancisco.

Bruner, J. (1987, Spring). Life as narrative: Reflections on the self. *Social Research, 54*(1), 11–22.

Brown, J. E. (1971). *The sacred pipe: Black Elk's account of the seven rites of the Oglala Sioux.* University of Oklahoma Press.

Brown, J. E. (2001). *Teaching spirits: Understanding Native American religious traditions.* Oxford University Press.

Carroll, A. K., Zendeno, N. M., & Stoffle, R. W. (2004). Landscapes of the ghost dance: A cartography of Numic ritual. *Journal of Archeological Method and Theory, 11*(2), 127–156.

Chapman, J. (2021). Didache. *Catholic answers.* www.catholic.com

Charles, M., & Rah, S-C. (2019). *Unsettling truths: The ongoing, dehumanizing legacy of the doctrine of discovery.* Inter/Varsity Press.

Costello, D. (2005). *Black Elk: Colonialism and Lakota Catholicism.* Orbis Books.

Clandinin, J. D., & Connelly, M. F. (2000). *Narrative inquiry: Experience and story in qualitative research.* Jossey-Bass.

Clow, R. L. (1990). *The Lakota ghost dance after 1890.* South Dakota Historical Society.

DeMallie, R. J. (1984). *The sixth grandfather: Black Elk's teachings given to John G. Neihardt.* University of Nebraska Press.

DeSersa, E. B. E., Pourier, O. B. E., DeSersa, A., Jr., & DeSersa, C. (2000). *Black Elk lives: Conversations with the Black family.* University of Nebraska Press.

DiAngelo, R. J. (2018). *White fragility: Why it's so hard for white people to talk about racism.* Beacon Press.

Douthat, R. (2018). *To change the church: Pope Francis and the future of Catholicism.* Simon & Schuster.

Dussias, A. M. (1997, April). Ghost dance and Holy Ghost: The echoes of the nineteenth-century Christianization policy in twentieth-century Native American free exercise cases. *Stanford Law Review, 49,* 773–852.

Ellis, C., & Bochner, A. P. (2011). *Autoethnography, personal narrative, reflexivity: Researcher as subject.* SAGE.

Enochs, R. (1996). *The Jesuit Mission to the Lakota Sioux: A student of pastoral ministry, 1886–1945.* Sheed and Ward.

Foley, T. W. (2002). *Father Francis M. Craft: Missionary to the Sioux.* University of Nebraska Press.

Foley, T. W. (2009). *At standing rock and wounded knee: The journals and papers of Father Francis M. Craft 1888–1890.* University of Oklahoma Press.

Frazier, I. (2000). *On the Rez.* Farrar, Straus, Giroux.

Ganguly, K., & Poo, M. M. (2013, October). Activity-dependent neural plasticity from bench to bedside. *Neuron 80,* 3, 729–741.

Goodhouse, D. W. (2019). *Makhoche waste, the beautiful country: An indigenous landscape perspective.* Master's thesis, North Dakota State University.

Goodhouse, D. W. (2019, December 21). Winter solstice is a sacred time. A time to carry one another. Mystic warriors on the high plains. *The First Scout.* http://thefirstscout.blogspot.com/

Grande, S. (2015). *Red pedagogy: Native American social and political thought.* Rowman and Littlefield. (Originally published 2004)

Greider, W. (1987, May 7). The heart of everything that is. *RollingStone,* 1–26.

Gustafson, F. R. (1997). *Dancing between two worlds: Jung and the Native American soul.* Paulist Press.

Holler, C. (1995). *Black Elk's religion.* Syracuse University Press.

Huel, R. (2003). Albert Lacombe. *Dictionary of Canadian Biography* (Vol. 14). University of Toronto/Universite' Laval. http://www.biographi.ca/en/bio/lacombe_albert_14E.html

Jacob, M. M. (2013). *Yakama rising: Indigenous cultural revitalization, activism and healing.* The University of Arizona Press.

Jacob, M. M. (2016). *Indian pilgrims: Indigenous journeys of activism and healing with Saint Kateri Tekakwitha.* The University of Arizona Press.

Jacobs, A. (2008). *Native American wisdom: A spiritual tradition at one with nature.* Watkins.

Jackson, J. (2016). *Black Elk: The life of an American visionary.* Farrar, Straus, and Giroux.

Jung, C. G. (1961). *Memories, dreams, reflections.* Vintage Books.

Kempis, T. A. (1999). *The imitation of Christ.* Bridge-Logos.

Kidwell, C. S., Noley, H., & Tinker, G. E. (2001). *A Native American theology.* Orbis Books.

Kolodiejchuk, B. M. C. (2007). *Mother Teresa come be my light: The private writings of the "Saint of Calcutta."* Doubleday.

May, R. (2019, January). Our lady of the Sioux. *Missio Immaculatae*, pp. 1–22.

Menakem, R. (2017). *My grandmother's hands: Radicalized trauma and the pathway to mending our hearts and bodies.* Central Recovery Press.

Neihardt, J. G. (1971). *Black Elk speaks: The legendary "Book of Visions" of an American Indian.* Washington Square Press. (Original work published 1932)

Neihardt, J. G. (1951). *When the tree flowered: The fictional, autobiography of Eagle Voice, a Sioux Indian.* University of Nebraska Press.

Neihardt, H. (1995). *Black Elk flaming rainbow: Personal memories of the Lakota Holy Man and John Neihardt.* Nebraska University Press.

Nerburn, K. (2009). *The wolf at twilight: An Indian elder's journey through a land of ghosts and shadows.* New World Library.

Oldmeadow, H. (2018). *Black Elk, Lakota visionary: The Oglala Holy Man & Sioux tradition.* World Wisdom.

Owens, L. (1998). *Mixed blood messages: Literature, film, family, place.* University of Oklahoma Press.

Palmer, P. (1998). *The courage to teach: Exploring the inner landscape of a teacher's life.* Jossey-Bass Publishers.

Portillo, A. (2013, Winter/Spring). Indigenous-centered pedagogies: Strategies for teaching Native American literature and culture. *The CEA Forum*, pp. 155–178. www.cea-web.org

Purzycki, B. G. (2006). Conceptions of humor: Lakota (Sioux), Koestlerian, and computational. *Nebraska Anthropologist*, 24.

Radin, P. (1972). *The trickster: A study in American Indian mythology.* Schocken Books.

Romero, D., & Wolfchild, C. (2017, January 25). Tiospaye. http://makingrelatives.org

Steltenkamp, M. F. (1983). *The sacred vision: Native American religion and its practice today.* Paulist Press.

Steltenkamp, M. F. (1993). *Black Elk: The man of the Oglala.* University of Oklahoma Press.

Steltenkamp, M. F. (2009). *Nicholas Black Elk: Medicine man missionary mystic.* University of Oklahoma Press.

Sweeney, J. M. (2021). *Nicholas Black Elk: Medicine man, catechist, saint.* Liturgical Press.

Taylor, M. W. (2012). *An autoethnographic journey to the self.* Doctoral dissertation, Marian University. (UMI 3553248)

Taylor, M. W. (2017, November 3). *The Dakota access pipeline educational experience: Embracing visionary pragmatism.* Paper presentation (for proceeding publication) to the 12th Native American Symposium, Southeastern Oklahoma State University.

Taylor, M. W. (2019, November 1). *The red and green "problem peoples": Shared cross-cultural affinity of Native Americans and Irish.* Paper presentation (for proceeding publication) to the 13th Native American Symposium, Southeastern Oklahoma State University.

Taylor, M. W. (2021, April). *Perpetuating joy in ephemeral and temporal affinity spaces through intercultural pedagogy.* Paper presentation to the University of Mary Faculty Colloquium.

Taylor, M. W. (2021, November 1). *Black Elk's life speaks: "That much...more."* Paper presentation (for proceeding publication) to the 14th Native American Symposium, Southeastern Oklahoma State University.

Taylor, M. W. (2022). *Perpetuating joy in affinity spaces through intercultural pedagogy.* Kendall Hunt.

Thiel, M. G. (2009, Winter). Catholic ladders and Native American evangelization. *U.S. Catholic Historian, Comparative Studies of Native American Catholics, 27*(1), 49–70.

Thiel, M. G. (2018, August 28). Three pamphlets by Father Henry I. Westropp, S. J., ca. 1906–1916. http//www.marquette.edu/library/archives/Mss/HRM/HRM-jesuits.shtml

Thiel, M. G., & Vecsey, C. (Eds.). (2012). *Native footsteps: Along the path of Saint Kateri Tekakwitha.* Marquette University Press.

Treuer, A. (2021). *Everything you wanted to know about Indians but were afraid to ask.* Borealis Books. (Original work published 2012)

Treuer, A. (2019). Personal communication regarding shared "affinity" among Native American and Irish.

Treuer, D. (2019). *The heartbeat of wounded knee.* Penguin.

Twiss, R. (2015). *Rescuing the Gospel from the cowboys: A Native American expression of the Jesus way*. IVP Books.

Vecsey, C. (1993). *Handbook of American religious freedom*. Crossroad.

Vecsey, C. (1997). *The paths of Kateri's kin*. University of Notre Dame Press.

Vecsey, C., & Venables, R. W. (1980). *American Indian environments: Ecological issues in Native American history*. Syracuse University Press.

Vizenor, G. (2008). *Survivance: Narratives of native presence*. University of Lincoln Press.

Warren, L. S. (2015, Summer). Wage work in the sacred circle: The ghost dance as modern religion. *Western Historical Quarterly, 46,* 141–168.

Zielinski, J. (2020). *Walking the good red road: Black Elk's journey to sainthood*. NewGroup Media.

Index

Printed in the USA
CPSIA information can be obtained
at www.ICGtesting.com
JSHW012026080824
67790JS00002B/8